After the Adoption

ELIZABETH HORMANN

After the Adoption

Fleming H. Revell Company
Old Tappan, New Jersey

Unless otherwise identified, Scripture quotations are from the King James Version of the Bible.

Scripture quotation identified TEV is from the *Good News Bible*—Old Testament: Copyright © American Bible Society 1976: New Testament: Copyright © American Bible Society 1966, 1971, 1976.

"Single-Parent Adoptions" is adapted from an article by Elizabeth Hormann which appeared in *Single Parent* magazine, March 1985.

Library of Congress Cataloging in Publication Data

Hormann, Elizabeth.
    After the adoption.

    Bibliography: p.
    1. Adoption—United States.   2. Parenting—
United States.   3. Parent and child—United States.
4. Children, Adopted—United States—Family
relationships.   I. Title.
HV875.55.H67   1987   649'.145   86-27992
ISBN 0-8007-1516-0

Copyright © 1987 by Elizabeth Hormann
Published by the Fleming H. Revell Company
Old Tappan, New Jersey 07675
Printed in the United States of America

TO Charlie,
my "child of the bulrushes,"
who has made adoption
such a joyous experience

Contents

One
Preparing for Adoption   15

Two
What the Experts Say About Bonding and Attachment   27

Three
Working Hard to Become a Family   35

Four
Adopting a Newborn   43

Five
Congratulations on Your Older Baby   57

Six
Adopting the Toddler: You Need Lots of Patience   66

Seven
The Preschooler: Not a Baby Anymore   77

Eight
The School-Age Child   90

Contents

Nine
Adopting a Teenager: Take One Day at a Time   102

Ten
Your Child Grows Up   112

Eleven
Forming Other Relationships   122

Twelve
Special Adoptions   131

Thirteen
Unusual Circumstances   145

Fourteen
What Is a Family?   165

For Further Reference   171

Additional Resources   175

Acknowledgments

Writing a book is a little bit like raising a child. The author, like a parent, has primary responsibility, but the credit for completing the project is never hers alone.

There were many contributors to *After the Adoption*. My children, Katherina, Madeleine, Charles, Irene, and Eli have taught me far more about family relationships than I thought I would teach them. It was my late father, Raymond A. Young, who first taught me about nurturing relationships. A desperate call for help with nursing my first child led me to La Leche League, a remarkable group of women who, more than twenty years later, continue to influence my mothering and form my primary support system.

In a large family, it is easy to find reasons not to write. My daughter Irene, at a time when her life was already full, took on a large share of running the household so I wouldn't have any more excuses.

My sister, Margaret Perkins, and her husband, Don, invited me to use their word processor, took care of the technical details, and sustained me with endless cups of decaffeinated tea and sandwiches. It was my sister too, who, nine months pregnant (and later with babe in arms) read through and corrected the entire text. Becky and Katie Perkins, my young nieces, reminded me that I do my best writing with children underfoot. My nephew, Danny Perkins, born at home during the word-processing phase of this book, was a delightful distraction and a reminder that there is more to life than getting things done.

Many people have influenced the way I think about relationships. The ones who have written books are acknowledged in the bibliography. Those who shared their thoughts in formal and informal interviews may recognize their influence in the text. I am grateful to all.

The female pronoun is used throughout the text to refer to the adopted child. Like the more conventional use of the male pronoun, this is purely arbitrary. Adopted children are, of course, just as likely to be boys as girls.

After the Adoption

One

Preparing for Adoption

In most cases the answer to "Why are you adopting?" may seem obvious. You want a child and, for reasons of infertility or preference, you are adopting one instead of making one yourself. But there is a deeper question behind this: Why is it that you want a child? That is not always so easy to answer.

What Are Your Real Reasons?

When people think about having a child, they often have a particular sort in mind. Some want a baby. They love the cuddliness and sweetness of an infant. They may imagine themselves with a magazine-perfect baby—clean, sweet-smelling, clothed in the latest baby fashion. If they are more realistic, they will know that babies are not always clean, sweet-smelling, or smiling. But if they are warm, nurturing people, they don't mind the messy details that go with the territory.

Some people think "boy" or "girl" when they say "baby." They are looking forward to the time when they can play baseball or go camping or rename the family business "Johnson and Son." They dream of braiding long hair, of closets full of Polly Flinders dresses, of prom dresses and wedding gowns for their little girls. Some men and women want a child to make their spouses happy, to give their parents a grandchild, or to provide a companion for a child they already have. Others want to rescue a child from physical or spiritual jeopardy. Some people, even in the late twentieth century, want a child so they won't be lonely—now or in their old age.

There are all sorts of reasons for wanting a child. The best of us have selfish reasons right alongside the more altruistic ones. It is all right to have some selfish motives. In the natural order of things, the human race continues because adults need to have children. But we are more than natural beings. We have a spiritual nature as well. Each child who is entrusted to us—by birth or by adoption—needs some measure of unselfish concern for her physical, emotional, and moral development. If we are to be good—even adequate—parents, we need to know ahead of time that our cuddly little babies will develop into headstrong toddlers, who in turn will be schoolchildren and (heaven help us) teenagers. Some of these stages will appeal more to some parents than to others, but all parents need to be prepared to offer love and guidance for the whole span of child rearing. It is a commitment, for better or for worse, to a person who will undergo profound changes in the eighteen years she is in your care.

If there is a stage you can't imagine tolerating, you might think of a project other than parenthood—or, if the stage is an early one, consider adopting children beyond that age. Fundamentally, *the only sound reason for having a child is your desire to raise her and nurture her through all the stages.* Along the way, she will almost certainly meet some of your needs as well—and just as certainly fail to meet some others.

Child rearing is a real adventure, often exciting beyond our wildest dreams, but also fraught with pitfalls and perils we hadn't anticipated. Only those hardy souls who are willing to see the project through—no matter where it takes them— should consider becoming parents.

Consider Your Expectations

Even the most realistic parents have expectations for their children, and both they and their children need these expectations to give them some sort of purpose as a family. Most of us want our children to be healthy, productive, loving people, and our child rearing is geared to help them develop that way. But most of us have hidden—or not-so-hidden—agendas of specifics for our children. We have come a long way since the first son automatically inherited the family business, the next one went to the church, the next into medicine, and so forth, but still we have dreams that we want our children to fulfill— often dreams we have not been able to fulfill ourselves.

The Role of Adoption Agencies

When you adopt through an agency, one of the purposes of the application process is to help you think through all the reasons you might want a child, to examine your expectations, and to come to a decision about whether or not you really want to be a parent. For people who do want to be parents, this process might help them look at children who are different from the ones they had imagined being theirs—or it might make it clear that they would be most comfortable with the sort of child they had planned on all along.

The application process can be a time of great growth, individually and as a couple. It can also be a time of great anxiety as you are scrutinized by relative strangers who will decide whether or not you can have a child. For the couple that has endured years of infertility treatment—all without success—this new scrutiny can be agonizing. It is almost unbearable to think of being turned down, not only because by this time the yearning for a child is so great but also because the need to feel successful is so important. In a culture that values precision fertility control—conceiving babies when you want them and preventing them when you don't—being unable to control your fertility is painful and humiliating.

Couples unable to conceive a baby suffer as much in the twentieth century as Sarah and Abraham or Elizabeth and Zechariah did when they couldn't have a baby. Adoption is a way to have a child to raise. It is *not* a way to cure infertility. Agencies sometimes have unreasonable expectations about a couple's acceptance of their infertility or about other aspects of their relationship or their hopes and plans for a child. And couples sometimes have to give the answers they know are expected if they hope to become parents.

Not being able to be yourself, feeling inhibited in exploring adoption openly, adds greatly to the natural anxiety prospective parents feel. Many agencies today are trying to redesign their process so clients feel less threatened. They are attempting to redefine the social worker's role as consultant rather than custodian of the keys to parenthood. When this works, the application process goes smoothly. Couples who decide to continue get a chance to look at themselves and their marriage in a way that encourages growth and commitment; both single and couple applicants can explore openly their fantasies and their hopes about having a child and, in this sort of atmosphere, prospective parents feel emotionally well-prepared for bringing a child into their lives.

The reality, though, is that the pool of potential parents vastly exceeds the number of children available for adoption through agencies—especially if the family is looking for a healthy white infant. Even if some applicants decide not to continue with the process—and some do—or consider another sort of child, perhaps an older child, a minority child, a child with handicaps, or a sibling group, there are still more applicants than babies, and there is a good possibility of being turned down or staying on the waiting list indefinitely.

Private Adoption as an Alternative

More and more, private adoption is becoming an alternative for families who can't—or don't want to—adopt through an agency. At one time, all adoptions were private. A child was orphaned; the neighbors knew a family that wanted a child, and the arrangement was made. Only in the twentieth century did adoption become the official process it is now. As social work developed into a profession and agencies took more responsibility for child welfare, private adoption declined and even became suspect. Eventually, private adoption was linked in the public mind with the buying and selling of babies—called "black market" adoptions—though, in fact, only the minutest percentage of private adoptions was illegal or in any way underhanded. Over the last decade, private adoption has begun to flourish again, in part because of the shortage of agency babies, in part because birth parents have begun to want a lot more involvement in selecting the people who will rear the babies they are bearing and relinquishing. Private adoption—legal in most states—can be accomplished in several ways.

The time-honored approach to private adoption is using an intermediary—usually a lawyer or a doctor. The intermediary knows of a couple who would like a child and of a woman who is planning to relinquish her child. The arrangements are made through this third person—in some states an adoption agency has to do a home study anyway—and there is no direct contact between the families.

Sometimes the pregnant woman goes to the intermediary with specific requests. If the intermediary arranges adoptions fairly often, he or she may have several potential families to choose from. The birthmother may be given some information about each of these families and then choose the one she believes is the most suitable.

Should You Make Contact?

The birthmother and the adopting couple may want to have some contact with each other. This contact may be by letter, passed through their intermediary. In these letters, both families can share as much of themselves as they choose and, in some measure, get to know the people who will be so significant in the life of a child they will both love. Adopting parents often use their letter in much the same way they would use the agency application process: to explore, with the person who most loves their baby, their plans and aspirations for raising a child. They may take advantage of this contact to get a complete medical history and a history of the birthmother's own family that they can later share with their child. Almost certainly, they will develop a strong sense of what sort of person is giving birth to their child, a clear understanding of why she is choosing to relinquish her baby, and an empathy with her that will help them present her sympathetically to their child.

One or both families may want a face-to-face meeting. This personal contact can be crucial in a birthmother's decision to relinquish her child comfortably, and to the adopting parents' ability to see her as a woman who made a difficult decision for the love of her child. Some families opt for a single meeting on neutral ground. They may use only first names. Other families are comfortable with more contact, with exchanging names, addresses, or telephone numbers. In some cases, the families grow so close that the adopting couple is invited to attend the birth. Suzanne Arms has explored this sort of personalized adoption, with it strengths and drawbacks, in her very moving book *To Love and Let Go* (Alfred A. Knopf, 1983).

Because confidentiality has been such a hallmark of American adoption, some families are uncomfortable with the idea of contact between the birthmother and the adopting family, but there are strong advantages to having contact—so strong that many agencies are beginning to experiment with incorporating it into their process. Personal contact of any sort generally leads to extensive information sharing. The adopting family becomes well acquainted with their child's background and gets a full medical and social history that can be useful—even vital—as they are raising her.

Adopting parents who know the birthmother as a person, even through a letter, are much better able to accept her and convey that sense of acceptance to their child. Adopted children as a group tend to suffer from low self-esteem, in part because of the prevailing view that their biological backgrounds are somehow unsavory. (A popular writer on adoption referred to birthmothers as "sexual aberrants," a designation that is as unkind as it is inaccurate. The child who perceives herself as having been born to an aberrant woman is not likely to feel very good about herself.) If adopting parents can share with their child their belief that the birthmother was a nice young woman who, in a difficult situation, made a courageous decision for her baby's well-being, the child will feel better about herself, her first family, and the adoptive family that empathizes so well.

The secrecy built into so many American adoptions encourages the fantasy that adopted children are born to their adoptive parents, that the experience of adoption is a totally joyous one in which a child and a family are brought together to live happily ever after. In fact, adoption grows out of some very painful experiences. A couple is unable to have children; a mother has a child she is unable to keep and a baby loses the mother whose voice and heartbeat and body rhythms she came to know and depend on in utero. The adoptive family tree is watered with a great many tears. Providing for some contact between the families ensures that that point is not overlooked.

Finally, contact with adoptive parents has strong advantages for the birthmother and, through her, the whole community. Women who have some role in choosing who will raise the children they cannot raise themselves generally don't suffer from the powerlessness and guilt that routinely plague women who have signed on the dotted line—often without even seeing their babies—and have been sent home with the admonition to "forget about it." They don't forget about it. They grieve terribly; they may feel regret and tremendous anger, or they may be withdrawn and depressed—sometimes for the rest of their lives. Some women hurry to have another child, often before they are ready for it. A few relinquish one baby after another; some never have another child. The ones who are unable to conceive after relinquishing may become adoptive parents themselves and, if their feelings over the lost child are not resolved, their families can have a very rocky road. We can't dismiss birthmothers as being of no concern to us. They don't just disappear to some remote island. For every adopted child—and adult who was adopted as a child—there is a birthmother. Most of them are alive and living right next door to us. She is our neighbor, the clerk in the post office, our child's Sunday-school teacher. All of our lives are affected if she can't get on with hers.

Getting Prepared

Whether you adopt through an agency or privately, it is a good idea to prepare yourself for the realities of being a parent. Reading some of the books on child development and parenting listed in the bibliography is a good start. Some agencies or communities offer parenting classes for prospective adoptive parents. "Borrowing" a niece or a nephew or a neighbor child is a good way to get some hands-on experience in the nitty-gritty of child care. Try to borrow a child who is not angelic to give yourself a more realistic picture. Some prospective adoptive parents are already involved with children as teachers, as youth group advisers, as coaches, or as scout leaders. If you are interested enough in children to make a commitment to children who are not your own, you will probably enjoy being a parent, but if you are adopting an infant, keep in mind that it will be quite some time before she can kick a soccer ball or fit into a Brownie uniform.

Extended families can sometimes be a problem in adoption. Their support is not absolutely essential, but life will go much more smoothly if they are at least open to the idea of an adopted grandchild (or niece or nephew). Sharing the process you are going through to become parents is often helpful to their understanding of why you are adopting and why there are children available for adoption. Some older people still believe that adopted children have "bad blood" because the majority of them are born outside a marriage. Your ability to portray the birthmother sympathetically may have a profound effect on the willingness of your parents and older relatives to accept your child. You need to be open, before you adopt, about your commitment to a child—even if your family is not accepting—and you need to convey that commitment, gently but clearly. Most families, given a little time, will make an effort to be accepting if they sense that it is going to be essential to maintaining warm family connections.

It may be especially difficult for grandparents to accept a child who is of a different race, who has a handicap, or who is already half-grown. Educating them to the need these children have for a home and the need you have to include this particular child in your family is part of the answer. If they are willing, including them in the preparations can go a long way toward helping them accept your child into the family. One single mother adopting from overseas had dramatic confirmation of this point. When her agency didn't notify her of her baby's arrival in time, she asked her father, who lived near the airport, to meet the plane. He called her back to report that the baby was beautiful, but he couldn't talk long because she needed him. He insisted on flying with the baby to her new mother's home and, the mother reports, "He hasn't missed an opportunity to see her since."

Your commitment to a child who is not a healthy white infant is even more vital than it is to any other child. Many of these children have already experienced a lot of rejection. They can't afford to experience it within your family. You could be faced with a painful choice if your family is adamant about not accepting your choice of a child. Try to make that decision before you bring a child into your home. It can be devastating to have to make it later.

Your other children, if you have any, will normally have been included in the adoption process, especially in an agency adoption. They need the same sort of preparation any expectant sibling needs to accept the changes that are about to happen. They need reassurances that they will still be loved just as much, and they need some sort of explanation about the birthmother. Children see things from a very self-centered viewpoint. This is not a character fault but simply reflects their developmental stage. When they hear about something happening to someone else, they wonder if it could happen to them. It is almost incomprehensible to a child that a parent could give up her own child. They need to be reassured that the birthmother's situation is totally different from yours, and that you would never relinquish them or the child you are planning to adopt.

Telling the children that the birthmother was very poor or wasn't married could become a problem in the future if your family has financial problems or loses one of the parents. It makes more sense to explain that the mother was very young, that she had not finished her education, that she was not grown up enough to raise a child. If you make it clear that raising a child is a project for a grown-up, and that grown-ups, even if they are single, have very little money, or are still in school, have the emotional wherewithal to raise a child, your children won't worry that their family stability could be jeopardized by a change in circumstances. If your child does not fall into the large category of children born to young, unmarried women, you need to share, to some degree, the situation she does come from. If your child has been abused, neglected, or rejected in a previous family, that needs to be shared in a way that encourages sympathy both for the child and for the parent who was unable to be loving and adult with her child. It is tempting to ignore the inconvenient reality that your adopted child was born to a woman who is not going to raise her. Don't give in to that temptation, even if your children don't ask questions. They are going to wonder and worry about it unless you offer some explanation.

Involving your children in the preparations for your new child encourages a family feeling about the adoption and commitment to the child being adopted. If the grandparents are hesitant about your project, the involvement of their grandchildren in it may be a powerful incentive for them to get involved too.

If you are adopting a child who is interracial, who comes from another country, or who has some sort of handicap (including the emotional handicap of being an older child), you would probably profit from joining a parent support group. In larger communities, there are active groups for parents of children with specific handicaps, for parents involved in international adoptions, for single adoptive parents, and for parents of interracial children. These parents know the potential problems and have solutions for many of them. They have already done the negotiating with the professionals and the community and their work can save you time, effort, and misery. If you don't live near enough to be active in a group, join one that has a newsletter and stay in touch that way. Most parents in these self-help groups are happy to talk with you by phone or correspond with you about the issues of raising the particular sort of child you will be adopting.

No amount of preparation can make us completely ready for all the nuances of committing our lives to another person.

Two

What the Experts Say About Bonding and Attachment

In the last few decades, we have learned a great deal about the way infants and parents normally make attachments to one another. In the mid-1970s, Marshall Klaus and John Kennell at Case Western Reserve in Cleveland, Ohio, published their findings from a small study in which some newly delivered mothers were given their babies for an extended period after birth and some followed the "normal" hospital routine. Their "early and extended" group had a chance for skin-to-skin contact with their newborns for an hour during the first two hours after birth, and on the next three days they had their babies for five extra hours each day. The routine-contact mothers saw their babies briefly at birth, again briefly six to eight hours later and, after that, every four hours for a twenty- or thirty-minute feeding period.

What Klaus and Kennell found supported their hypothesis of

a "sensitive period." A month after birth, the extended-contact mothers were more reluctant to leave their babies, did more soothing of a fretful child, and looked their babies directly in the eye more than the mothers with routine contact. A year later, the extended-contact mothers still did more soothing and stayed in closer contact with their babies and, in a study of a small selection of these same mothers and babies two years after birth, the children in the extended-contact group scored significantly higher on IQ and language tests.

Changes in Childbearing Practices

In their book *Maternal-Infant Bonding* (Mosby, 1976), Klaus and Kennell drew together research from all over the world that supported essentially the same position: that the timing, the kind, and the frequency of contact a mother has with her baby after birth can have a profound influence on the quality of their contact throughout the child's infancy.

Publication of this research came as childbirth and parent-education groups were becoming widespread and were beginning to have some influence on the medical management of pregnancy and childbirth. Klaus and Kennell's work was welcomed in these groups and served as a catalyst for dramatic changes in childbearing practices. Natural childbirth, which had been growing steadily in popularity since the 1950s, was much more acceptable in light of these new findings. A mother needed, after all, to be alert if she were going to have this sort of early interaction with her baby.

Fathers came into the delivery room in droves so they could be a part of the early minutes of their children's lives. Even when the birth was by cesarean section, more and more parents insisted on being available emotionally to their child right from the start. Birthing rooms, "gentle birth" (with dim lighting, quiet surroundings, and a bath for the baby to ease her transition from the world where she had floated comfortably in her mother's womb), and home birth came more and more into vogue.

Despite a simultaneous technological push which made ultrasound, amniocentesis, and fetal monitors a part of "normal" birth and shot the cesarean section rate up to 50 percent in some areas, low- or no-intervention births with high parent-baby contact became a respected and sought-after way of giving birth and a means to early and strong family bonding. Postpartum rooming-in and breast-feeding continued the emphasis on bonding-oriented care.

Prenatal Influence

Tom Verny, in *The Secret World of the Unborn Child* (Dell, 1982), took things one step further back in the process with his reports of prenatal influence on both the physical and emotional development of a baby. His information about the physical effects of drugs and chemical exposure during pregnancy is fairly well known. What is not so well known is the effect of stress and the concomitant variations in hormonal output. Recent research has made clear what pregnant women have realized intuitively: Babies in utero are sensitive to their mothers' moods. They react to loud noises, to pressure or prodding from the outside, to music and strong lights. Their sensory apparatus functions actively long before they are born. And once they are born, they recognize the familiar voices and body rhythms of their mothers and "remember" sounds and experiences they have had in the womb.

Verny cites some pretty remarkable—and well-documented—stories that add emphasis to his research: the orchestra conductor who "knew" numerous pieces on sight, even though he had never seen them before. This man's mother was a cellist and, to everyone's surprise but hers, the pieces her son knew were the ones she had played during her pregnancy with him. Or the newborn who mystified everyone by firmly rejecting her mother's breast while eagerly latching on to the breast of another woman. It came out in an interview that her mother had not wanted to have her and had, in fact, continued her pregnancy only because her husband wanted her to have the child. The baby, Verny hypothesizes, was protecting herself from rejection she had already experienced in the womb.

New Ways of Looking at Child Care

Researchers like Verny and Klaus and Kennell have opened up some pretty exciting possibilities for nurturing babies and their relationships with their parents practically from the moment of conception. A baby is hardly a "little stranger" but a small person who is already known in many respects and already knows her mother—and perhaps her father as well (there is some evidence that babies recognize their fathers' voices too, if they have heard them regularly during the pregnancy). The new birth practices—when they are available—and the greater awareness of the importance of touch in child rearing have begun to alter both professional recommendations and child-care practice in many families.

But there has been a dark side to this movement as well. When families have not been able to use these new insights in their childbearing—and up until ten or fifteen years ago, the overwhelming majority of births in this country were not conducted along these lines—they often feel guilty and totally responsible for any problems their children may have. The potential pool of guilty parents is enormous: parents of children over fifteen, cesarean and bottle-feeding parents, parents of premature or ill babies, and adoptive parents are all vulnerable. For a variety of reasons, most of them beyond the parents' control, the prenatal life, the births, and/or the early weeks of their children's lives did not go smoothly. Undeniably, there is some sense of sadness and some loss in these experiences. But it is all too easy to move from acknowledging this loss and sadness to assigning blame for it. It is ironic, but not too surprising, that these new insights and research which have enhanced the lives of so many families can, when they are turned around, feed right into our most widely played parlor game: Blame the Mother (and sometimes the Father too).

Adoptive parents who, quite often, have not been winners in the Fertility Sweepstakes and have had to prove their "parent worthiness" with both endless patience and exposure of their private lives to more or less public scrutiny, may be more vulnerable than most parents to feeling guilty and responsible. It is vital for the well-being of the whole family to get some perspective on the subject of bonding.

The Importance of Touching

In the Klaus and Kennell study, there were several factors involved in "extended contact." Timing was only one of those factors. These mothers had their babies more often and for longer periods than the mothers who had routine contact and they were encouraged, by being presented with undressed babies, to have skin-to-skin contact. Routine-contact babies would ordinarily be presented in clothes and wrapped in a blanket. It is fairly common to discourage mothers from unwrapping their babies (though, in fact, most of them do, at least once). The more obvious attachment behavior of the mothers in the extended-contact group probably came about as much from the quality and length of their early contact with their babies as it did from the timing of that contact.

The need to be in touch does not go away in the first few days after birth. Ashley Montagu, in his ground-breaking book *Touching: The Human Significance of the Skin* (Columbia University Press, 1971), made this quite clear. Babies, young children, not-so-young children, and adults need to touch and be touched by other human beings. Tactile deprivation in infancy and young childhood prevents both physical and emotional growth. Older children and adults who for some reason stop being touched lose something vital to their mental health and will often go to great lengths to replace it.

Adoptive parents and their children generally do miss out on the early days, weeks, or months together, but that does not mean they won't be able to form an attachment to one another. In principle, the attachment is made the same way it would have been had the child been born into the family. Parents and child need to spend a lot of time together at frequent intervals, and some of that contact should be in the form of touch. Just exactly how these principles are worked out in practice will depend on the child's age and temperament. Clearly, it is not appropriate to sit in the rocking chair with a teenager, but you can see that she gets plenty of hugs and that you are in touch with her in the casual way you are with your other children: a touch on the hand, shoulder, or hair when you talk to her; a kiss hello, good-bye, and good-night.

It is not too difficult to be convinced of how important touch is for babies and young children. The power of touch to soothe a fretful baby is legendary. A healthy baby delights in the touch of someone she knows and trusts. She snuggles down, drapes herself across shoulders, wraps herself around legs. She solicits touch by reaching for the people she loves, and she communicates by touching everyone and everything with her hands, her feet, and her mouth. If her efforts to touch and be touched are rebuffed, she is thoroughly miserable. She lets you know that being touched is not an optional activity in her book. If a child is not touched or is rebuffed too often, she may appear to "outgrow" that need, but it doesn't disappear. It just goes underground. The child who suffers tactile deprivation will soothe herself by sucking her thumb or fingers, pulling at her toes or fingers, twisting her hair, rocking back and forth, banging her head, or doing some other repetitive behavior. If she has grown accustomed to meeting her needs with one of these behaviors, she might even be resistant to being touched by other people, but that is what she needs nonetheless.

Touching can be not only growth-producing but healing as well. Early in Matthew's Gospel, Jesus' healing of Peter's mother-in-law is described: "And he touched her hand, and the fever left her" (Matthew 8:15). Later in the same Gospel, a woman is healed by touching Jesus: "For she said within herself, If I may but touch his garment, I shall be whole" (Matthew 9:21). He goes on to the ultimate healing, raising a young girl from the dead: He "took her by the hand, and the maid arose" (Matthew 9:25). The Apostles healed by touch, and laying on of hands to heal broken bodies and spirits is widely practiced in the church today.

If we expect healing by a single touch from people who are often strangers to us, why doubt that we can heal our children with touch that is repeated day after day? Healing is a gift of the Holy Spirit promised to us all. We have not been promised that healing will be instant or that it will seem miraculous to all observers. The promise we have is that the laying on of hands, done lovingly and prayerfully, brings to the people we touch—and to us—the healing power of the Holy Spirit. What Montagu, Klaus, and Kennell tell us in psychological terms is what we have known all along by faith.

Touch is one part of the picture in bonding to our children. Time and attention are the other parts. We can't just tuck our children into the corners of our lives. They need to be somewhere in the center labeled "Essential Business." Child rearing is very time-consuming and it should not be filled just with the minutiae of caring for them physically: cooking and laundering, dressing and undressing, picking up after them, and providing the material things they need (or want).

Children, the Bible tells us, are the gift of God (Genesis 33:5). If we cherish them as we should, we need to give them our attention. The Apostles became impatient when some parents tried to bring their children to Jesus to be blessed. Jesus had important things to deal with. His disciples didn't want Him bothered with children, but "Jesus called them unto him, and said, Suffer little children to come unto me, and forbid them not: for of such is the kingdom of God" (Luke 18:16). In that one brief exchange, Jesus told His disciples to get their priorities straight. Children were not a bother and a distraction to the real business He was about; they were central to it.

A Chance to Become a Family

Most societies still tend to be modeled, in that respect, on the Palestine of Jesus' time, but in the smaller society of the family, that does not have to be the case. Children need to feel that they are important to their parents, that their parents have time for them and that they have their parents' full attention when they need it. Adopted children, by virtue of the disruption they have experienced in their original bonds, may have an even greater need for their parents' time, attention, and loving touch than most children. It may take them longer to trust and to form attachments, but with patience and persistence, most adoptive parents are able to help their children feel loved and feel safe loving in return.

In the past, adoptive families, encouraged by professional advisers, have expended a great deal of energy in maintaining the fiction that their families are no different from families that are bound together by ties of blood. But adoptive families *are* different. Every member of an adoptive family is acquainted, to some degree, with loss and grief. Out of that loss and grief, an opportunity to become a family is created. Carefully nurtured, the bonds in an adoptive family are strong and long lasting, the delights well worth the difficulties.

Three

Working Hard
to Become
a Family

In light of all the research on early—even prenatal—bonding, adoptive families may, understandably, worry about being able to form the kinds of bonds with their children that are necessary for healthy emotional growth and an affectionate family life. But as we have seen, timing is only part of the story. We make strong bonds with people later in life. For instance, our best friends and our spouses are usually people we meet well beyond our infancy. Sometimes we make these connections in nursery or grade school; more often these bonds aren't formed until high school, college, or well into our adult lives. Our understanding of bonding research and our experience of making attachments beyond infancy can help us figure out how bonds are forged in adoptive families.

Our children do not come to us as blank slates—not even the children we make ourselves. From the moment they are conceived, they have a complex set of genetic predispositions. The prenatal environment they experience and the interaction (or lack of it) with the mother who will give birth to them, gives shape to their psyches as well as their bodies. The relationships adoptive children have had with other people before they come to you also play a role in developing the person who is your son or daughter. You can't recapture the time you missed with your child, but you can build on the good things that were begun and fill in where there are gaps.

Getting to Know Each Other

Any new child, homemade or adopted, needs substantial time with her parents if she is going to grow attached to them and they to her. If you are a two-career family or a single parent, arranging for your new child to have contact with you pretty nearly full-time for a while may be difficult, but it is an important investment in your future as a family. Children learn to love by being in intense touch with one or two other people at first. They can branch out later, but first they need to get to know you and grow attached to you. That takes time.

We understand this principle when we schedule honeymoons for newly married couples, but in late twentieth-century America, the idea of prolonged intense parent-child contact has fallen out of favor. Middle-class mothers who once routinely stayed home to care for their small children are now expected to fit in the demands of those children around the (more important) demands of a career. Parental leave, a routine prerogative in every other industrialized country in the world, has not caught on much in the United States. But the needs of young children do not wait upon social reform. Any young child needs frequent access to her mother or father, and the more disruptive her life has been, the more vital this contact is going to be. If you are planning to adopt a child under school age, try to have one parent home most of the time for several months. Newly adopted school-aged children will also do better in their new families if there is a parent available to them when they are not in school.

If there is no way your family can arrange for a parent to care for your child full-time, consider having her cared for by one other person rather than in a day-care center. Small children are easily confused and overwhelmed by the numbers of people, both adults and children, who are, by necessity, at a day-care center. Give her a chance to form her primary attachments before you confront her with a bewildering array of new people. Even a part-time nursery school may be too much for her until she is well settled in your home. If she has been in preschool and can continue in the same one, it might be a useful transition for her, but changing schools or starting school afresh at the same time she moves into a new home might overwhelm her and make her adjustment more difficult.

Find a Style That Suits Your Family

Your physical presence is going to be very important in the way you interact with your newly adopted child. You will be able to act more appropriately with her if you have some understanding of child development. A simple guide to the stages of development will give you a rough outline of what you can expect at her age, in terms of both skill and behavior. Add to that a couple of good books on child-rearing approaches, some observations of other children her age, and some discussion with experienced parents whose style—and children—you admire, and you will be off to a good start in understanding your own child.

As you consult the experts—both the professionals and the parents in the field—listen to your own instincts too. No one ever corners the market on child-rearing methods. Find ways that are comfortable for you and your child. If your son or daughter and your family are thriving on the methods you use, you have probably chosen an appropriate and effective parenting style. That style might vary a good deal from the style your parents used or the ones your neighbors swear by, but you aren't trying to find a style for all families. Developing one that suits your family is enough.

What You Can Expect

Unless your child is an infant, you can expect that the disruption in her early life will have caused some alterations in her developmental timetable. Moving into your home is probably going to "throw" her for a while too. She may be exceptionally good or she may behave exceptionally badly the first few weeks, until she settles in and lets you get to know her real self. Don't expect too much during this adjustment period. She is getting to know you and the way your family runs; you are getting to know her and the way she runs. Once you have gotten well acquainted, you will have a better idea of what you can expect of her and what you can't.

Realistic expectations will make it much easier to set goals and settle on some child-rearing methods that will help her blossom into the person she is meant to be, but you don't have to wait until you fully understand her (you might wait a long time for that—with any child) before she can begin to flower.

Understanding is only one part of the picture. Love is a very vital ingredient, and something you can share and she can feel from the very first day. Even if you don't "bond" with her instantly and "fall in love" with this new child, you can treat her in a way that she can recognize as loving. We tend to think that loving behavior grows exclusively out of loving feelings, but that is only half true. It is just as likely to work the other way around. The more we act in a loving way, the more likely it is that our feelings of love will grow. Just as feelings can flow from the inside out, they can also flow from the outside in.

Lots of Hugs and Attention

Young children "catch" your loving messages most easily with direct contact. They need to be held and talked to and nuzzled and sung to every day, several times a day. This may come spontaneously to you and if it does, you will have no trouble with it. If you think you are not a "natural" hugger and cuddler, you have probably learned somewhere along the line to avoid physical contact with other people. It is not healthy and not something you want to pass along to your child. Human beings need to be in touch—literally—with other human beings if they are going to be healthy emotionally. In psychiatric circles it has become common to prescribe four hugs a day as a preventive measure against mental illness. This is a bit tongue-in-cheek, but the principle is sound. People thrive on hugs and wither in their absence.

There is good reason to believe that many adolescents and single adults are sexually active even if they don't particularly enjoy it or like their partners because they need to be touched. If their families aren't physically demonstrative, or if they feel that affectionate displays are out of place at their age, adolescents may be starved for human contact and may get it in an inappropriate way. Even younger children may not get enough physical contact. If they have been deprived in their earlier months, their need to be touched may be insatiable. Some children will even entice their parents to spank them because they are so desperate to be touched. Try to respond when your child reaches out to you or asks to be held. Don't worry about spoiling her. When she feels safe and secure in your affection for her, she won't need to be so demanding. Putting her off or rationing out your hugs too much will only prolong the time she is so needy.

Your child not only needs your touch; she needs your attention as well. This may, on the surface, seem to be the same thing, but it isn't. We have all held our children absentmindedly while we talked on the phone or visited with a neighbor. In fact, it is very often the times when we are busy with something else that our children come and solicit some attention. Even absentminded holding is better than no attention at all— and sometimes it is sufficient. We are, after all, people too, with interests, needs, and responsibilities of our own. Our children don't have to have our undivided attention every waking minute. In fact, it isn't good for them to think they can or should have it. But they do need some periods of concentrated attention, some time when you aren't doing or thinking about something else, some time that is just for you and your child. If your child is old enough to talk, she needs you to listen and respond appropriately; she needs to share her dreams and her disappointments, tell you stories, and try out her ideas on you. If she isn't yet talking, she needs to have you talk to her and make a fuss when she tries to "talk" back. These one-way conversations are a crucial part of her learning to communicate.

Your daughter needs to do things with you. The child who plays patty-cake with you will be the same child who plays Scrabble (and wins) a few years down the road. Teach her to cook and you will have a companion in your kitchen. Let her teach you to knit and she will have reason to feel competent. Share your interests in biking or bird-watching, in swimming or singing, in hiking or handicrafts, and you are developing her sense of mastery. Eventually there will be another pair of helpful hands in the house.

It is tempting, once our children have mastered a skill, to keep them busy with chores or activities while we go about our business, but that is not what they want or need from us. If they are going to develop and strengthen their bonds with us, they need us to share in many of the things they are doing and they need to share in the activities that interest us (as well as the ones we *have* to do, even if they don't interest us). There is a place for independent activity and there is merit in helping children learn to amuse themselves, but it can be overdone.

Families are not just clusters of people leading independent lives under the same roof. If they have joint activities and projects, if family time and "alone" time are routine parts of the schedule, then you will have a family that nurtures the children as well as the adults who live in it.

Bonding Is Hard Work—and Well Worth It

In the best of all possible worlds, children are wanted and born to parents who are able to take care of them. But we don't live in the best of all possible worlds. Not every child who is conceived is wanted or can be cared for by the parents who conceived her. Not everyone who would like to have children is able to make them. Even when children are born to parents who love and care for them, there can be a tragedy that deprives those children partially—or entirely—of their parents.

Children become available for adoption for many reasons, and for just as many reasons, adults want to adopt these children. But any adoption is a compromise of sorts. There is always some sadness or a tragedy in the background that made adoption a possibility.

When we are tempted to use the "chosen child" approach in telling our children about adoption, we need to remember that it is somewhat misleading. We do miss something by not knowing our children from the moment of birth (or before) and they miss something too, by being separated from the mother whose heartbeat and voice and body rhythms have been familiar to them from the first days in the womb. It is not easy to form bonds with strangers—especially if there have been many separations and broken relationships in the past. But it is this very background of sadness and loss that gives adoptive families such intense motivation to make their adoptions work.

Children in adoptive families know at some level that they need their parents and can't take their presence for granted— and parents, too, need their children in a way that parents who can conceive a child at the drop of a hat do not. Even parents who have biological children know how lucky they are when a child becomes available for them to adopt, and they are usually eager to make up for lost time, whether that time is measured in days or in years. This heightened awareness of their good fortune, this sense of specialness, are strong motivators for the whole family.

Adoptive families work very hard to become families and because of their strong commitment are often even more successful at it than families who acquire their children by birth. Most adoptive families, by necessity, get a late start at bonding. They may have to try a little harder and be a little more flexible, but the vast majority of adoptive families establish ties that are as strong and as satisfying as any in a family that is connected with blood ties.

Four

Adopting a Newborn

In virtually every respect, adopting a newborn is the ideal way to begin. While there is some evidence that babies are already well acquainted with their mothers in utero and can, in the first few days, distinguish them from other mothers by smell, the bond is not as intense as it would be later on. Newborns are reasonably adaptable and usually bond well to their adoptive parents. The heartbeats and voices of their new parents quickly become familiar sounds they love to hear. If they are held frequently, they learn to recognize these parents by touch and smell, and it is the adoptive parents they first know by sight. When an infant's physical and emotional nurturing needs are consistently met by one or two people, those people become the real parents, regardless of the circumstances of birth.

Parents, too, attach most readily to a newborn. While we know that no baby, however young, is a totally blank slate, by virtue of their brief time in the world, newborns don't carry with them traumatic histories or deep attachments to other parents. The adoptive parent with even a modest understanding of infant needs is likely to be well received by the baby, to feel competent very early on, and to grow attached very quickly.

A Large Dose of Cuddling

Babies make their first contacts with other people through touch. They need to be in frequent—sometimes constant—physical contact with other people if they are going to form attachments and learn that they are lovable and loved. This runs counter to the child-rearing theories that were popular a generation ago, but the research is pretty unanimous on this point. Babies need plenty of body contact to thrive both physically and emotionally. At minimum this means holding the baby for all of her feedings, picking her up each time she cries, and holding her until she has settled down again. It means stroking her hair and her skin, rocking her, gentle play, and all-around cuddling right from the start—every day. For many families this will mean a baby carrier or a backpack is more important than a carriage, that the bassinet gathers dust while the baby is tucked into her parents' bed, that a Bathinette or baby tub is superfluous because the baby feels safer held by a parent or sibling for a bath.

Don't expect universal acclaim if you choose to stay so closely in touch with your baby. You can expect to be warned against "spoiling" the baby, against "overexciting" her, against "wearing yourself out." You will probably have to contend with a variety of old wives', old doctors', and old psychiatrists' tales about the physical and emotional dangers of sleeping and bathing with your infant. Keep in mind that infants have the most intense need for physical contact. Meeting those needs with "marsupial mothering" is entirely appropriate at this stage. As she grows she will *want* to be more separate *if* you have met her early need for closeness. If you are going to feel secure, you need to do your research (some of it has been done for you in the bibliography) and be prepared to share it with the people who are trying to give you advice. You will want to be tactful, especially if your would-be advisers are family members or professionals whose services you might need later on. A simple "thank you for your concern," a referral to something you have read—or even a copy of a pertinent passage or article—and a firm reminder that *you* are the baby's parent is tactful enough.

Persistent or intrusive advice givers may need a more direct approach. It is vital to choose an approach that you are comfortable with, support yourself with the information you need to carry it out, and tune out, as much as possible, the people who might undermine the kind of parenting you are trying to do. Unlike many parents, you had to qualify for the job. More than likely, you have the skills to do it as long as your confidence isn't eroded.

Sleeping Patterns (or Lack Of)

Sleeping and feeding are usually the biggest concerns for parents of a newborn—not surprising, since those are the newborn's primary activities. There is a myth, developed during the era of "scientific" child rearing, that babies sleep twenty-two hours a day—at least most of the time. That is hardly ever true. Babies drift continually among several stages of consciousness. A baby in an apparently deep, quiet sleep can move quite suddenly into a more active but still-sleeping stage, or may just as suddenly be wide awake and alert. Initially, she listens only to her own body rhythms and may seem to be awake—or asleep—all day (and night). Babies are catnap specialists. It takes most of them several weeks (or months) to develop sleep/awake patterns that approximate the routines in their families.

Everyone hears stories of babies who slept through the

night from their first night at home. Occasionally that is true, but there are several other possible explanations. The definition of *through the night* can vary. In some households, a baby who sleeps four or five hours after 11:00 P.M. is considered a "through the night sleeper." In other families, a baby who has slept through once or twice is counted. Her almost daily "relapses" are overlooked. Some parents identify their babies as "good sleepers" to keep potential critics at bay. In families where parents and young children sleep in the same bed, the baby might wake up fairly often and drift right back to sleep, comforted by the warmth and closeness of her parents. The parents may not even realize she did wake up.

Some babies, sadly, learn in the first few days or weeks that it is no use crying when they wake up. No one is going to come anyway. Maybe they sleep through the night, maybe not. If they sleep in a separate room and have been taught that crying gets no response, their parents will assume they sleep through, whether they do or not. A newborn baby who regularly sleeps out of body contact with other people is probably not getting enough handling. Rousing her or moving her into the parents' bed will ensure that she is touched enough for normal physical and emotional development.

At first, babies don't make any distinction between day and night. They sleep when they are tired, regardless of what is happening around them. A lot of parents worry about "getting them on a schedule" and this is not a totally unreasonable concern. Even though babies' needs are quite immediate, there are things that must be done if the household is going to function. Parents and other children need to eat. A change or two of clothing, a few clean towels and sheets, diapers, and clean dishes have to be available. The house can look "lived in," but it should not attract the attention of the local health department. Even these minimal jobs take time, which may be hard to find in a household where the baby never sleeps.

Letting household tasks go or letting the baby cry it out are not solutions that promote happiness in the family. A baby carrier that allows an adult to do a few chores while a baby naps and gets her body contact can be a lifesaver. The gentle motion of a cradle or a windup swing can hold some babies for a short while. When both parents are home, one can hold the baby while the other does some of the necessary jobs, or an older brother or sister can be helpful in that respect. A simple plan for accomplishing the routine chores can make it much less overwhelming and can free the parents to enjoy this brief time when the baby needs to be plastered to their person almost round-the-clock.

Parents are sometimes tempted to race around and work like crazy when their fitful sleepers do take a nap, but this ensures that the parents get no rest and no time to themselves. This is the time to unplug the phone and take a nap yourself, read a book, or have coffee together like real grown-ups. Smart parents whose fitful sleepers will sleep regularly only when attached to another person, turn necessity into a virtue. They find a comfortable place, put on their favorite record, lay out a snack and a book within easy reach, and, *voilá*, baby's nap time becomes time for mother to restore herself too. This time will be relatively short. Soon enough, the baby will be able to sort out day and night. She will be less restless and she will sleep more soundly for longer periods. Nothing quite matches the delight of a baby falling asleep in your arms—and waking up smiling when she discovers that you are still there. It is one of the joys of early parenthood that we too often miss in our eagerness to "get things done."

If you would like to nudge your baby along a little in the direction of sleeping more at night and staying awake more in the daytime, you can try waking her every couple of hours during the day. See that she is fed, warm, dry, and tucked up comfortably before you go to bed. She may pick up your day/night pattern a little sooner than she would have left to her own devices—or she may not—but eventually she will figure out the difference and conform her schedule more or less to the one in the household.

Feeding Is Much More Than That

Eating is the second great concern for parents of newborns. Most adoptive parents will bottle-feed their babies, at least partially (nursing the adopted baby is covered in the next section). For all babies, feeding is a way of nurturing both body and spirit. The *way* in which babies are fed is just as important as *what* they are fed. Above all, they need to be held for every feeding. Propping the bottle "just this once" is very tempting in a busy household, but taking this sort of shortcut cheats both the baby and the parents of important time and interaction together.

A newborn may appear not to notice. She may feed very intently, with her eyes closed, and finish up the feeding sound asleep, but she knows if she has been held. She is aware of the heartbeat, the voice sounds, the smell and feel of the person holding her. If she is propped, she knows she is by herself and she gets a message that most parents don't really want to send.

Very early on the baby will begin to interact with the person feeding her. She will hang onto a finger or a piece of her parent's clothing; she'll interrupt her sucking to look into her mother's eyes or to smile at her father. If you are not there—in body or spirit—you'll miss this, and so will your baby. If you aren't there on a regular basis, a very important avenue of communication with your baby will be closed off.

The best way to hold your baby while you are feeding her is cradled tightly in one of your arms. This way she has the maximum body contact, she can hear that you are there, and she is close enough to focus on your face. If she is fed with her head in your lap, she is too far away to hear your heartbeat and too far away to realize there is a face there she could be smiling at.

Feeding time needs to be leisurely. While most babies can get all the milk their bodies need in ten or fifteen minutes, not all babies can, and ten minutes is not adequate time to get the emotional nurturing they need as well. Generally, a baby will suck quite vigorously at the beginning of a feeding, then stop for a while to rest or burp or snuggle into her mother's (or father's) arms. The baby who stops sucking to smile and play with your hands or your clothing is not "fooling around." She is building a relationship with you, getting to know you and helping you get to know her. Feeding time is social time and cuddling time as well. There is no place in a baby's life for "drive through" meals.

What you feed your baby will be decided jointly with your medical caretaker. Today most bottle-fed babies use some sort of commercially prepared formula, but canned milk, goat's milk, and soy-based formulas are also in common use. If you have a complete medical history on your baby, you may be able to anticipate better if she is likely to be allergic to milk and decide on formula accordingly. Goat and soy milk are commonly used for allergic babies. Fresh cow's milk is generally avoided in the early months to prevent allergic reactions. Milk is really all most babies need the first four to six months. The American Academy of Pediatrics does not recommend the early start on solid foods that was so common a generation ago. In part, this is an allergy preventive; in part it is just good sense because babies don't develop the enzymes they need to digest many of the starchy "starter" foods until sometime in the middle of the first year. Early solid foods can be a poor nutritional choice when they are used as a substitute for the milk a baby really needs. This practice has also been linked to childhood (and adult) obesity.

How you feed the formula is a matter of choice. Some parents swear by the old-style bottles and nipples that have been around for most of this century. Other parents prefer to use nipples that are designed to be more "natural"—softer or contoured to match more closely the way the mother's breast would fit into the baby's mouth if she were breast-feeding. It probably makes sense to get just a few of each kind to try them out unless you are sure what you—and your baby—will like best. The important criteria are nipples that require the baby to suck vigorously (this promotes jaw development) and a flow that is neither painfully slow nor so fast that the baby chokes and splutters her way through the feeding.

Nursing Your Adopted Baby

While the vast majority of adopted babies are bottle-fed, more and more of them are being breast-fed—at least partially. In a culture which still regards breast-feeding a home-made baby as an iffy proposition, nursing an adopted baby can seem a strange and impossible task. It is not impossible, but it is not easy either. Adoptive mothers have to expect their experience to be different from what it would have been with a homegrown baby, but for many mothers it is a satisfying alternative to bottle-feeding.

Normally, the lactation process is quite simple. The end of a pregnancy signals the breasts to start producing milk. The baby's suckling signals them to continue producing. Prolonged and frequent sucking will produce milk even in a woman who has never been pregnant, but there are some pitfalls en route. During a pregnancy, the milk ducts enlarge and the body is primed hormonally for lactation. When a baby starts nursing "from scratch," there is a lot of catch-up work to do. With enough sucking, the hormonal process will be triggered even without a prior pregnancy and the milk ducts will gradually enlarge. In the meantime, there are the problems of feeding a hungry baby and keeping her interested in nursing until the milk starts to come in.

There are a number of solutions, but the approaches that make the most sense involve making some mental distinctions between this experience and the one that a mother who had given birth would have. The terms *nursing* and *breast-feeding* have somewhat different meanings. Understanding the distinction can make all the difference in the kind of experience an adoptive mother has nursing her baby. A nursing baby sucks frequently at the breast. She enjoys it and so does her mother. Nursing is about a relationship. A breast-fed baby gets all her milk from the breast. She and her mother may enjoy it—or they may not. Breast-feeding is about eating. A nursed baby may be totally breast-fed or she may get no mother's milk at all. (In practice, a homegrown nursed baby is almost always totally breast-fed as well.)

A nursing baby and her mother are in a relationship that helps them grow attached to each other. The baby nurses for the sheer delight of it, for comfort, to go to sleep, instead of using a pacifier or a thumb and, in the process, she learns that her source of warmth, comfort, and affection is her mother rather than some inanimate substitute. In the process of nursing, the baby will stimulate her mother's breasts to make milk, and eventually she will be breast-fed as well—at least partially—but that is secondary to the relationship.

How do you get a baby to suck at the breast? It is easier than you might think. A newborn will suck instinctively and even a slightly older baby needs only a little teaching. Babies don't know they are supposed to get milk every time they suck at the breast. (Nursing babies often nurse long after they have fed, even though there may be only a trickle or an occasional drop of milk.) They quickly learn to use the breast as a pacifier, if their mothers structure the situation carefully.

An adopted baby who is going to be nursed should go to the breast at every opportunity. She can nurse while her bottle is heating and when she is finished feeding, she can go back to the breast to nurse to sleep. It is not so different from using a pacifier to keep a hungry baby quiet or to get her back to sleep. When she is restless and cranky, nursing can soothe her; when she needs to unwind to go to sleep, she can unwind at the breast. She may nurse a little when she wakes at night and not get up until she is really hungry. The possibilities go on and on, but the heart of it is, put the baby to breast anytime you might otherwise consider using a pacifier. Try to get her to the breast at least every couple of hours during the day to provide enough stimulation to start the milk flowing, and to enjoy the relationship you are building with her.

While most adoptive nursing mothers use bottles for feeding at least some of the time, there are mothers who prefer not to, and for them there are alternatives. Most common are devices to feed the baby at the breast. Marketed under a variety of trade names, they are constructed from plastic bags similar to those in some nursing bottles, or solid plastic, a stopper, and fine tubing. The bag is filled with formula and attached by a clip to the mother's clothing or hung by a cord around her neck. The fine tubing goes to nipple level. As the baby sucks at the breast, she is also getting formula from the tube. Some mothers describe it as "sort of like having your milk ducts on the outside of the breast instead of the inside."

Some mothers, because of personal preference or severe allergy in their babies, use donated mother's milk in these feeders, but donated milk is hard to come by and most mothers use formula instead. Some adoptive families use a homemade version of these feeders: the original one was designed by an adoptive father for his wife to use while nursing their baby. Some feed their babies by spoon or cup and use the nursing to ensure that the baby gets enough sucking. Many families use a combination of these methods.

Milk, while a secondary issue, is of concern to most mothers who are nursing their adopted babies. It is hard to predict just how much any adoptive mother will produce, but there are some general guidelines. Most likely to have a good milk supply is the mother who was already nursing one baby when the adopted baby arrived. She is well primed, and it is just a matter of extra sucking to produce extra milk. Women who have recently—within the previous three months—weaned a baby, had a stillbirth or late miscarriage, or have given birth to a baby who did not survive, are the next most likely candidates for an adequate milk supply. It might take a little longer, but their bodies have not yet reverted to prepregnancy state and they have a biological edge over many other women.

Women who have never been pregnant or who have not been pregnant or nursing within six months before their adopted baby arrives are just about equivalent, biologically speaking. When they begin to nurse, they are starting from scratch. A study of these women showed that they reach their peak nursing time within three to four months after they begin, and by that time they are producing, on an average, about half of what their babies need. That means, of course, that some are only producing a quarter and others have about three-quarters of the milk they need. The only women in this study who didn't have any milk at all were women with pituitary defects which prevented their becoming pregnant. Two women, neither of whom had ever been pregnant, had full milk supplies. Both of them had pumped their breasts for many months before the baby came.

Pumping is a fairly simple technique in which the breasts are stimulated by hand or with a breast pump. The milk ducts in each breast are compressed gently and rhythmically for several minutes each. Because this mimics a baby's sucking at the breast, the pituitary gland is signaled to start producing milk. Most women begin pumping two or three times a day. Some women may prefer to follow a schedule similar to a baby's own—every two or three hours.

Preparation might seem to be the key to a good milk supply—and certainly it is worth a try—but there are some things to keep in mind. Pumping—even a great deal of pumping—doesn't always produce the same results in different women; nothing quite matches a baby's sucking for the correct sort of stimulation. Stimulating an abundant milk supply requires an almost fanatical dedication to pumping. Most women don't have the time to dedicate themselves so fully to this pursuit and, because the arrival of most adoptive babies is so uncertain, pumping can turn into a long-term and discouraging project. The focus on milk supply can detract from the focus on a relationship which is, after all, the whole point.

There are studies from other countries indicating that women in cultures which generally support breast-feeding produce milk more easily and more abundantly for their adopted children than do women in Western societies. There has been some largely unsuccessful experimentation with chemical aids to starting up lactation. As we understand more about the way lactation works and as our society becomes more accepting of breast-feeding as the natural way to nurture a baby, both physically and psychologically, adoptive mothers will probably produce more abundant milk when they nurse their babies. Even now, most mothers of newborn adopted babies who want to do it can establish a nursing relationship. For the bulk of women who have approached it with reasonable expectations and some support, it has been an experience they wouldn't have wanted to miss.

One mother related her satisfying nursing experience: "Nothing I had read or talked over, not even seeing other women at La Leche League meetings nursing their babies, prepared me for the joy I felt when my baby nursed. She became mine in a special, irreplaceable way. All the hard work and patience at the beginning was worth it when she finally figured out what to do—and liked it. It is still, years later, a source of great delight to remember that tiny person nestled in my arms, sucking for all she was worth, stopping now and then to smile or look around, then drifting off to sleep, still nursing. This time in our lives was sheer bliss."

For more information on nursing your adopted baby, *see* "For Further Reference" and "Additional Resources" at the end of this book.

Getting Acquainted

Most newborns—even those adopted by single mothers— have other relatives to get acquainted with besides their mothers. While they need to make a strong attachment to one or two primary people (usually the parents), there is room in their lives for brothers, sisters, grandparents, and assorted other people in the general category of family. Most fathers today don't need to be urged to be involved with their babies, but they may need a little encouragement to try their hands at skills they didn't develop when they were growing up: bathing, changing, and dressing a baby, rocking her, giving her a bottle.

In most families, the mother still stays home during the early weeks and does much of the baby tending, at least during business hours. Many fathers enjoy doing it in the evening—even during the night—but may hesitate to volunteer. Fathers need to be in touch with their babies just as much as mothers do if they are to form an attachment to them, so it is a good idea to encourage participation right from the start.

Fathers can also fill some roles that mothers might have difficulty filling. Dad can screen phone calls and visitors the first few weeks, just as he would if Mom had given birth. She may not be recovering from a pregnancy, she may not have had the work of labor and delivery, but she *is* caring for a newborn baby. She is losing sleep and she is getting to know a new person.

Just as couples need a time alone to get acquainted and become a couple, so do families. The first few weeks should be a time for the parents to spend time with their baby and limit their contact with people outside. This doesn't mean grandparents have to wait weeks to meet their new grandchild, or that there should be no calls or visits from other relatives or friends, but they need to be in moderation. Sometimes a husband is better able to say that—and be heard. Husbands can be good screeners of advice, especially important for the first-time mother who is a little unsure of herself, or the nursing mother who is being deluged with commentary on her "crazy" project.

Brothers and sisters need to be involved with the new baby. Time-honored sibling tasks, like fetching a clean diaper and entertaining the baby, are useful, but they also need to be closely in touch to bond well. Even very small children can hold a baby with supervision. Older siblings can have a little more responsibility than younger ones, but it is important not to overburden them with premature parenthood. What you are looking for is building a bond and creating a feeling that family making is something everyone does together. You do that best by making the contacts between siblings and the new baby as pleasurable as possible.

Extended family also attaches best by being physically in touch with the baby. In families which have not had adopted children before, this may be particularly important to overcome any lingering doubt about opening up the family to people (even little people) not related by blood. It is a rare person who won't bond to a baby with whom she has spent an afternoon in the rocking chair. Getting family involved without letting them take over can be tricky. You might want to plan ahead so you'll have a tactful reason not to leave your month-old infant with Grandma (or anyone) for the evening, a gracious way to turn away intrusive questions about your baby's background, a nice approach to ignoring advice you haven't asked for. You want to establish that *you* are the parents, but at the same time you want to make other family members feel their involvement is welcome.

Don't Expect Too Much Too Soon

A new baby, especially a first baby, is a big adjustment for any family. When the baby is adopted, tensions may be particularly high, in part because the wait to become parents has been so stressful, in part because the baby is, in a very real sense, "a little stranger." If you expect to bond instantly with your baby or feel deliriously happy now that your long wait is over, you may be disappointed. Relationships with babies, like relationships with other people, take time.

As you get to know your baby by being in touch with her, she won't seem such a stranger. As your skill in caring for her and reading her signals grows, your confidence will grow too. In time you won't be able to imagine life without her. Gradually, almost imperceptibly, the bond between you will have strengthened, and she will have become your very own child.

Stranger anxiety is common to all babies at this age, and for this baby, her adoptive parents, no matter how lovingly they welcome her, are at first strangers. She may resist being touched and respond very little or not at all to overtures to make her smile. She may cry a good deal. She may sleep an extraordinary amount when she first comes—in part from the exhausting strain of separation and newness, in part from depression. Or she may not sleep at all. Her appetite may be off or it may be voracious.

Babies vary as much in the way they show sadness as older children and adults do. However she behaves, it is safe to assume that your baby is missing the people who cared for her and will need some time to mourn before she can form an attachment to you. Like newborns, older babies develop an attachment best by being in touch with their parents. It is possible that you might meet some resistance from an older baby who is not used to being touched or who is apprehensive about being in touch with a stranger (you). Sometimes these babies are seen as "good" babies. They sleep long hours, they don't demand much attention when they are awake, they may even prefer to hold their bottles themselves.

It is sometimes tempting to leave these babies to their own devices—after all, they are no trouble, and compared to babies who cry constantly, they certainly are a pleasure to have around. But don't be lulled by how "easy" these babies are. They need to be touched; they need to interact with the people in their families. Independence is not a healthy quality for an infant. A baby who prefers to be alone and doesn't enjoy being touched is in trouble emotionally.

One experienced adoptive family had just such a baby. When she came to them at one year, she was very withdrawn and shrank from their touch. Recognizing at once that her tolerance for being touched had to be increased, they used a baby carrier for much of the day and slept with her at night. At first she resisted all their attempts at closeness. In bed at night she drew herself up as far away from her parents as she could manage. But over a period of weeks, she relaxed. She no longer pulled away from their touch and even came to enjoy it. Eventually—and much to her family's surprise—she began to indicate that she wanted to nurse as she observed her sister doing. At thirteen months she became a nursing baby, but that was just a bonus to the really important accomplishment of getting in touch with and bonding to her family despite some clear and serious early deprivation.

Normal babies do have different requirements for intimacy with other people. Some babies are, in fact, more reserved than others by nature. But it is important to recognize the line between healthy reserve and withdrawal.

By contrast, some babies seem open and friendly from the start. Their adoptive parents report "no problem" in their adjustment to their new family and, indeed, there are babies who are very adaptable, who have been so secure that they can reach out fairly easily to new people. You don't want to search needlessly for pathology, but at the same time, you probably do need to be concerned if your baby never shows the slightest distress at being separated from her early caretaker or, as she settles in to your home, from you. She may need some help in learning how to make a real attachment. This sort of baby needs lots of time with one or two people with only minimal separation—none at all, if you can manage it for a while. She needs a continual pattern of interaction with lots of touching that she can count on and trust. Only then will she be able to form a significant attachment to you. It is important to her later ability to care for other people that she make an exclusive attachment early in life.

Get Some Background Information

One of the best aids to integrating an older baby into your family comfortably is a detailed account of her life to date, her schedule (if any), her sleep patterns, feeding patterns, food preferences (if she has started solid food), the way she has interacted with the foster family or caretaker she has had up until the time she came to you. If she has had more than one caretaker, a history from all the previous people who have cared for her will help you assess how she adapts to change and where you need to concentrate your efforts. A birth and health history will also help you understand her needs. Ideally, some means of being in touch with the foster family—even through an intermediary—during the first few weeks might help you fill gaps that appear over that time.

Should You Nurse Your Older Baby?

Babies need a certain amount of consistency. Changing families is plenty for most of them to absorb at once. If they are used to a particular formula or are on solid foods, try not to change these at first—even if you have different nutritional preferences. It goes without saying that the baby who is attached to a pacifier or a "blankie" should continue to have it even while you are teaching her to turn to you for comfort. Changes can be made gradually as she becomes comfortable in your home.

While a baby under three or four months old is considered the ideal candidate to become a nursed baby, a lot of babies begin at a later age. There are frequent reports of babies between six and nine months learning to nurse, and the baby mentioned previously was considerably older than that. In theory, there is no reason it shouldn't be possible. Mothers routinely wean their babies from the breast at this age and teach them to drink from a bottle. Teaching a bottle-fed baby to nurse is the same process in reverse. The baby is being asked to learn a new sort of sucking and, biologically speaking, at this age she is capable of learning it. The problem lies in the interpretation mothers put on their babies' behavior when they are in the learning process. A nursing mother who is trying to wean her baby to the bottle expects a certain amount of resistance. After all, she is asking the baby to learn something new and to give up something she likes. She knows she will have to be patient and that many attempts to use the bottle will end up with her nursing the baby instead. She also knows that if she is gentle and patient, the baby will eventually try out this new piece of equipment—just as she will later learn to use a cup and spoon and fork. The mother doesn't take her baby's resistance personally.

On the other hand, the mother who is trying to teach her baby to nurse after being bottle-fed for several months may not accept her baby's resistance with such equanimity. It is hard to see that the baby is rejecting the change and the new equipment when that change and that equipment is such an intimate part of the mother herself. It feels like a personal rejection—even though it really is not. The adoptive mother has to have extraordinary patience and a strong self-concept to see her older baby's early behavior at the breast for what it is, and to persist in offering to nurse her. Again, the point here is that *nursing should enhance the attachment between mother and baby.* There is no point in setting up a situation that is going to diminish the mother's self-esteem and make attachment more difficult.

Nursing is simply a part of the overall program to get in touch with your baby. If it doesn't become comfortable fairly soon, it doesn't need to continue. Parents try a variety of ways to get in touch with their babies. Some of them work; some of them don't. When something isn't serving its purpose, dropping it from the program does not mean failure. For families who have already been disappointed by infertility, it is particularly important not to structure the situation in a way that might be perceived as another failure.

Lovingly Handled

Brothers, sisters, and extended family can be encouraged to bond to an older baby in much the same way they attach to the newborn—and it might even be more fun because older babies "do things" and can be played with. People aren't so afraid of handling a baby who can sit up and crawl, and they enjoy the greater responsiveness that these babies normally have. This is the good side of adopting a slightly older baby who has been lovingly handled. She is more fun and more interesting. She may also have sleeping patterns that fit the family's style more closely than a newborn's (but don't count on it). She is probably finished with colic and if she is six months old or more, she may be just about ready to start eating some meals with the family.

Most babies can start right out with table foods if solids are started in the second half of the first year. Feeding them may not be any tidier than feeding a very young baby jarred baby food (especially if you encourage them to finger feed themselves), but it is a lot more fun because they are old enough to take pleasure in different tastes and textures.

The baby at midyear will reach milestones one after another: sitting up, pulling to standing, crawling, waving "bye-bye." By nine or ten months, some babies are already walking and using a few simple words. It is easy to track their development at this stage and to feel competent as parents. Each new stage elicits the praise and adulation a baby needs to feel competent and loved.

You and Your Shadow

Probably the biggest problem with a healthy baby in the first half of the second year is separation anxiety. Once the baby has made an attachment to you, she may be loathe to let you out of her sight. Even stepping around the corner to answer the phone or to get a fresh diaper may elicit howls of protest from her. If she is mobile, she may crawl after you as fast as she can and wrap herself around your leg to keep you in her sight. It is a trying stage, but one you can expect with any baby—homemade or adopted. It is actually a positive sign (though it may not feel like it) that your baby has bonded to you and that she has developed intellectually enough to know whether you are there or not. What hasn't developed is her memory. She has difficulty holding you in her mind when you are out of sight, even for a minute or two, and she can't remember that you always come back. It takes time for these skills to develop. In the meantime, your baby may prefer to see life plastered to your person.

It is important to reassure your baby with your behavior that she is, in fact, safe, that you are, in fact, dependable, and that you take her concerns seriously. Keep your separations very brief—just long enough to throw a load of wash in the dryer, then reappear. Let her follow you if she can, or carry her along if you are going to be gone more than a minute. This may be a time in her life when she really can't tolerate having you gone or when she is comfortable with only one or two other people. You don't need to worry about spoiling her by giving into her need. If you meet her need for your presence now, she will be satisfied, and as soon as she remembers that you do return, she will be able to let you go more gracefully.

For a baby who has already lost one or more caregivers, the extra effort to make her feel secure can be crucial to her willingness to trust and to reach out later on. Cope with the intensity of her needs by designing your life around her. This is the time to invite people to come to your house instead of going out (unless they welcome the baby too). If she is comfortable in your arms or a backpack, you can take her along on your visits to the museum, to an outdoor concert, or to a play (or sit in the back at one that is indoors). Find a church that doesn't mind a little baby noise during the service (and sit in the back there too, in case her volume gets too high).

It is a short time—even though it can feel very long when you are going through it. This might not be the best time to put her in a room of her own. She may well be more comfortable continuing (or starting) to sleep with you. You are not creating sleep problems by responding to her need to be in touch with you during the night. Many adults have difficulty sleeping if their partners are away. Babies are able to tolerate isolation even less well.

If baby is a restless sleeper, she can sleep on a separate mattress or futon (a foldable mattress for the floor) in your room at least part of the night. Even if she sleeps in a room of her own or with a brother or sister, she may have difficulty getting to sleep and may wake more than once during the night. Letting her cry it out only teaches her that no one will respond to her needs. If she needs to be held or rocked or nursed to sleep, feel free to oblige her. Nobody needs these things forever and the better you meet her needs now, the more easily she will grow out of them. A lot of children don't sleep soundly through the night until they have gotten all their teeth—at about two or two and a half years old.

Older babies like to interact not only with the people around them but also with the objects in their environment. This is the beginning of "getting into things." For the parent who is just establishing a bond with an adopted baby, it may be difficult to figure out how to set limits without jeopardizing their fragile attachment to each other.

Not Naughty—Just Curious

The easiest way to deal with the "getting into things" stage is to remove as many temptations as possible. Electrical outlets need covers, wires need to be anchored firmly out of reach. A lock against toddler incursions isn't a bad idea. Precious items such as breakables, good books, and records look better at your eye level than at the baby's anyway.

Most parents will want to avoid the frustration one young mother experienced when she continued to keep her books— carefully alphabetized—at baby level. It took weeks of daily alphabetizing her collection before it dawned on her that her life and her baby's would be easier if the books were stored somewhere else. The fewer temptations, the less you have to say no. When an "attractive nuisance" is unavoidable, distraction is the name of the game—and at this age it is generally pretty effective.

There is no place in baby rearing for hand slapping or yelling—though it can get mighty tempting sometimes. Babies don't have much capacity for self-control. They aren't bad; they just haven't developed enough to control themselves. They can learn to be afraid to do certain things, but that is not the message we want to give them. A baby needs an active parent willing to provide an environment that is safe for her to explore and willing to remove or distract her from things that are not safe. It is the parent who provides the self-control in the early months. Only very gradually, and in a loving atmosphere, can the baby learn to control her impulses herself.

Making a healthy, well-cared-for baby part of her new adoptive family is usually not an extremely difficult job. Separation from the first family can be an issue, but parents who are sensitive to this issue can usually help their baby get through her sadness at losing the first family and her fear of letting her new family out of her sight. Babies at this age are generally very appealing little people, easy to love, easy to attach to, and relatively easy to integrate into the adoptive family.

Six

Adopting the Toddler: You Need Lots of Patience

A toddler can be roughly defined as any child who walks upright but isn't yet ready for nursery school—a child somewhere between one and three years old. This is a time of tremendous growth and change. At the beginning of the toddler years, the child still toddles (thus the name) unsteadily on her feet. By the end, she runs quickly and surely and has enough coordination to ride a tricycle. New toddlers can say very few words. By three years old most children are talking in full sentences; in bilingual households they can do it in more than one language. One-year-olds are still very eager to keep their mothers in sight; three-year-olds are often ready to enjoy an independent life—for a couple of hours, at least. Perhaps it is this independence that is most characteristic of the toddler stage. They want to learn things, they want to try out new skills, they want to do it themselves, and they want to do it

66

their way. They are a source of great delight—and despair—to their parents, who alternately enjoy watching their growth and are exasperated by it.

Parents who have raised their toddlers from infancy have a lot going for them to help them over the inevitable humps. They are, by this time, strongly attached to their children and know to some degree what makes them tick—and the children have an equally strong attachment to their parents (though that may be hard to discern during their most negative moments). Mutual attachment, the parents' skill in handling their child, and the child's clear preference for a parent when she is in a tight spot make managing the challenging behavior of a toddler less difficult and more palatable. The child who is adopted as a toddler, and her family, have to get along without these built-in helps. It can be rough going for a while.

Your Toddler Needs Acceptance

The newly adopted toddler is not yet attached to her new parents. More than likely, she was attached to the old ones, and their loss is as painful to her as it is inexplicable. She is hurt, grieving, angry, trying to reach for independence just as all her familiar supports are taken away. A lot of toddlers react angrily, living up every inch to the reputation of a terrible two-year-old. They are very difficult to manage and may not fulfill any of their parents' fantasies—at least not at first. Other toddlers withdraw, become depressed, and show regressive behavior. The more traumatic the change in their lives, the more likely they are to behave in this way. They are easier to manage than the children who act out, but they don't fulfill their parents' dreams either.

As one mother told me: "We had been prepared for our two-year-old to be sad leaving her foster family and coming to us, but her anger took us by surprise. I had imagined rocking her in the same chair that rocked generations of babies in our family, but she wanted no part of it. She had tantrums in the day and woke up with nightmares at night. It was very difficult watching her grieve and rage and not being able to comfort her. Eventually she did turn to us and eventually we all felt better, but it was a rough start."

Parents adopting a toddler need realistic expectations, a high tolerance level for behavior that would normally be unacceptable, and lots of patience. They need to understand that, at a critical point of her development, their new child has to accept the loss of parents to whom she is attached, adjust to totally new surroundings and people, and develop an attachment to strangers she did not select as her new parents. It is a tall order for a child who is between one and three years old.

The first step to making the toddler part of your family is accepting her, no matter how unappealing her behavior. You may have been waiting for her for years, but she hasn't been waiting for you. It is going to take her a while to realize what a good thing she has. Accept her acting out or withdrawal for what it is. She is grieving and she is scared. Her whole world has turned upside down and she is responding to the changes out of limited understanding. Her behavior at this point cannot fairly be labeled "bad." Her behavior may understandably disappoint you, but as an adult, you need to be able to understand why she is acting the way she is and to convey to her your acceptance of her as a person and your commitment to draw her into your family.

Affection Is Important

You'll draw your new daughter in best by concentrating on some of the bonding mechanisms discussed in the last two chapters. Even if she is resistant at first, she needs to be touched. You might be more successful at getting her to enjoy it during familiar activities like bathing or dressing. An extra stroke of her hair and a quick hug are easy to sandwich in between the business details of these projects. Games like "patty-cake" and "this little piggie went to market" are opportunities to be in touch in a way that she will probably enjoy. Later on, some gentle tickling might be welcome. Holding her on your lap to play games with her toes, tie her shoes, or read her a book will probably be more acceptable at first than trying to rock her.

Some toddlers respond better through an intermediary. They will sit close in order to hold the new kitty, or they will accept a hug and a kiss from a teddy bear that they would reject from you. You touch children of this age with your words as well as your hands. Eventually, they will respond to words of affection and gentle encouragement to get close.

Because her guard is down when she sleeps, this might be the best time to get in touch. The baby who has drifted off in her car seat may sleep on, rocking in her mother's arms or curled up next to her in bed. You may think she doesn't notice, but she does. Her acceptance, at an unconscious level, of your affection as she sleeps will in time blossom into a conscious acceptance of it when she is awake. It takes time, patience, and ingenuity to build trust.

You also build bonds with a toddler by involving yourself in her activities and inviting her to join you in yours. Even the toddler who firmly rejects your involvement in playing Lego (and any toddler will do that) can usually be enticed to "help" when you are baking cookies. She may enjoy digging beside you when you are gardening, and quietly join in when you play your aerobic dance music. If she has had a reasonably stable and loving environment before coming to you, her curiosity to learn about her new environment will, sooner or later, overcome her fear and her hurt at losing the environment she used to have. If she was not nurtured well in her first year, she will probably need more time before she can readily involve herself in activities with you.

Your toddler may bond first to a sibling or a grandparent.

Her pain at losing her first parents might make it difficult for her to reach out to you. Some toddlers show a distinct preference for one parent over the other, and take a very long time to warm up to the less-preferred parent. The accepted parent needs to understand how terrible a rejected parent can feel, support that parent's continued efforts to reach out to their child, and gently encourage the child to get acquainted with the parent she doesn't like as well. If the parents are quietly, patiently persistent, their child will eventually grow to love them both.

What to Do Ahead of Time

Some of the difficulties of the transition from one home to another can be alleviated by having some preplacement visits. These are routine with older children, starting at around two and a half years of age, but they may not even be considered for the young toddler—the very person who probably needs them the most. The toddler who has had a chance to get to know her new parents before her move to their house is much more likely to seek them out for comfort when she is hurting. If she has been in foster care, it makes sense for her to get acquainted with her new parents from the vantage point of her foster mother's arms. Foster parents can offer a tremendous amount of information about the baby's life to date, her schedule, her likes and dislikes, and the behavior that is typical of her.

It can be useful for the adoptive parents to have access to the foster parents for a while after placement. Very often, the child does better if she can phase in her move to the adoptive family and gradually phase out her involvement with the foster family. This takes a little more time and effort for both families and sometimes for the social worker as well, but it can be a wonderful help to the child in making a smooth adjustment—and the well-being of the child is, after all, the whole purpose of adoption.

Structuring Versus Limiting

Next to bonding, the most important thing you can do for your toddler is to help her learn limits. Many parents don't look forward to this time in their children's lives because they imagine it as a period of continued battling and *no* saying (on both sides). It doesn't have to be that way. Toddlers do not test limits because they are bad but because they are trying, in their immature way, to learn about the world. A toddler who is well attached to her parents is as eager to please them as she is to explore. Parents can help her learn the rules of the household and the outside world without having continual confrontations if they structure things carefully. As you plan this structure, keep in mind that the purpose of setting limits is to keep your child safe, to help her learn how to live within the family, and later on, with people outside the family. At this age, there is no need to set limits solely for the purpose of character development. There are enough limits that come up in the normal course of her life to ensure the beginnings of good character development.

In some areas—primarily matters of safety—parents need to structure the environment so a slipup in the toddler's self-control won't put her in grave danger. Rigorous child proofing is essential. Anything she might eat—soap powder, medicines, vitamins, cleaning supplies, plants, newspapers, cigarettes, matches, thumbtacks, money—needs to be out of reach at all times. "Most of the time" isn't good enough because toddlers move fast and head for familiar items you leave lying around. Because you never know when your toddler will become a climber, it makes sense to store anything that is potentially dangerous behind locked doors. Child locks are available commercially and while you are buying them, pick up several packages of plugs to put in empty outlets. If outlets aren't sealed off, your toddler will more than likely experiment by putting her finger or a match box car in the hole and get a nasty shock.

Stairwells need to be locked off until your toddler can negotiate the stairs in both directions, and even afterward if you don't want her going where the stairs lead. A chain lock very high up on each door—beyond the reach of a toddler standing on a chair—will prevent untimely escapes. On the other hand, you will probably want to remove the locks in the bathroom, your child's room, and any other room or closet she can get into, or you will become well acquainted with the fire department's rescue service.

It goes without saying that toddlers need constant supervision in the bathtub, on the playground, and wherever they are that is not totally child proofed. From their very first ride in the car with you, they need to be in a car seat that safely restrains them (not all car seats are safe), and they need to observe that you use your seat belt every time you drive. Holding hands crossing the street should be routine, even as you are teaching them to look both ways.

With a very young toddler, it is foolhardy and frustrating to have all your precious breakables and your books accessible. She needs an environment where it is safe to touch most things and where there are not too many *no's*. As she gets a little older, she will be better able to understand the idea of being careful, of having respect for precious things, and of not touching what is not hers. Then you can begin to leave these things within reach.

Once you have created a safe environment with a bare minimum of nontouchables, you can begin to help your toddler learn which things are hers and which are not, which things may be touched and which things need to be left alone. Distraction is your best tool with a toddler. If she is touching your books, offer her one of her own with the comment that this is *her* book. If she sees you writing out your check and wants to join in, give her paper and crayons to do her work beside you. If she wants to help when you are cooking, give her a bowl and spoon of her own while you use the mixer (and don't let her see you put your finger in the bowl while the mixer is going). She is always ready to imitate you. Giving her alternatives is a lot easier on both of you than constantly saying no—and this is how you help her develop a large repertoire of acceptable activities.

If your daughter won't be distracted, you may need to move her out of temptation's way. Try to figure out why she is refusing to be distracted. She might simply need some attention. If you can manage it, it will save time and frayed nerves in the long run if you give her the attention she is asking for. She may be hungry or tired. A wholesome snack—some cheese, fruit, a few whole wheat crackers, or yogurt—might be just what she needs, or perhaps a brief nap might be in order. Be careful about distracting by feeding or putting her to bed, though. Take the time to sit down with her while she eats or to sit beside her while she falls asleep so she won't feel pushed off. It can set a very unwholesome pattern if she begins to use food or sleep as a substitute for your attention.

Sometimes a toddler just won't be distracted from something she really should not do. That is when we are likely to call her "willful." Maybe she is willful or maybe we just can't figure out what the problem is, but in any case she can't be allowed to do something that could really hurt her, or someone else, or damage property. She may need to be removed from the place that is tempting her so much, and she probably won't be very happy about that. This is where things can escalate.

Thwarted toddlers are not known for accepting the inevitable graciously. An emotionally healthy toddler will protest noisily. She may kick and scream and strike out at anything in her path. She may bang her head on the floor and emit anguished wails that attract the attention of all and sundry in the general vicinity. She may, in short, have a temper tantrum and a parent, frantic to quiet her down, may have a temper tantrum of his or her own, complete with screaming, slapping, and all kinds of threats if the child doesn't stop right now.

Usually, by this time, the child is not able to stop. First, she didn't get what she wanted; then she got out of control and when she counted on her parent to help her get back in control, Mom or Dad got out of control too. A parent who is raging and hitting isn't disciplining her child, no matter what she calls it. She is not putting the fear of the Lord into her. She is simply terrifying her. Parents need to remain adults, even in the scary presence of a child in midtantrum.

A child having a tantrum desperately needs someone to help her recover her balance. She needs to be protected from hurting other people and things—or herself—and she needs to be in the presence of an adult who is calm and confident that she can regain control. The parent who picks up her screaming toddler (remove her shoes first; you'll feel safer), holds her tightly—even if she resists—and speaks to her in a calm tone, is going to quiet her down much more quickly than the parent who joins in the fray. It is up to the parent to keep the focus on the real issue: that the child can't have whatever it was she wanted, and no amount of screaming is going to alter that. If she is yelled at or hit for having a tantrum, all she is going to learn is that grown-ups are allowed to express their angry feelings—even have tantrums—and children are not.

As she grows older, the toddler's tolerance for frustration will grow and, if she has been handled lovingly, she will learn to protest in a more civilized way, eventually even to accept a *no* gracefully (sometimes). Parents are responsible for helping their children develop self-discipline, but many parents expect too much at an early age and worry too much that negative behaviors, normal at this developmental stage, will continue and escalate unless they are dealt with ruthlessly. They perceive wickedness where there is really only immaturity. Children need guidance, but that guidance is most effective when it is done with a gentle hand.

A Word About Spanking

Toddlerhood is the time when many parents begin to wonder about the role of spanking in raising their children. Proverbs 13:24 is very often quoted, not only to justify spanking but also to "prove" that God intends for children to be spanked. In the King James Version of the Bible, it does appear that way: "He that spareth his rod hateth his son: but he that loveth him chasteneth him betimes." The Good News Bible, however, has a different flavor: "If you don't punish your son, you don't love him. If you do love him, you will correct him."

There is a lot of room for discretion when you think in terms of correcting children. Many parents don't feel good about spanking their children, especially such small children. The important point is that we guide them and correct them when they go astray. It should not be our purpose to make them pay for every infraction. That is vengeance, and on that the Word of God is clear in any version: "To me belongeth vengeance, and recompence . . ." (Deuteronomy 32:35), and "The Lord will take revenge and punish them" (TEV). We need to help little ones learn the household rules, the community rules, and God's rules—by word, by example, and when necessary, by correction, but correction needs to be gentle, or all they will learn is fear and resentment.

Most parents don't want their children to fear them or harbor resentments against them, but our fears and inexperience can sometimes lead us down paths that are filled with danger to our relationships with our children and to their healthy development. Spanking, used as a regular means of disciplining a child, can be one of those dangerous pathways. The occasional spanking—the sort most parents administer almost instinctively when their child has done something terribly dangerous, like running out into traffic—is not going to do any harm (and probably not much good either). Children need to know their parents are human too, but they also need to feel that their parents love and cherish them and have their best interests at heart. That is a hard notion to convey if spanking is a regular part of discipline.

Toddlers in any family can be a real challenge. They need to try their wings and begin the long, slow journey toward independence; at the same time they are very small and inexperienced people who remain almost totally dependent on their parents. Conflicts—within themselves and with their parents—are inevitable. The recently adopted toddler may experience greatly intensified conflicts as she tries simultaneously to attach to and separate from her new parents. Compound this with grief, anger, and fear at being separated from her previous caretakers, and the need for extraordinary compassion and patience becomes clear.

Seven

The Preschooler: Not a Baby Anymore

The toddler and the preschooler overlap in some ways, but preschoolers generally are firmly established as children, not babies. Both their gross motor skills (walking, running, and climbing) and the fine motor skills (crayoning, manipulating Lego pieces, and dressing themselves) are pretty well developed. They are (mostly) toilet-trained, and sucking needs that dominated the earlier years are on the way out. Some of them continue with the pacifier, the bottle, the thumb, or the breast, but usually in a very limited way. Other things are much more interesting to the child between three and five.

The parent who adopts a preschooler is thrust into the busy and expanding world that characterizes this age group. Many children this age already attend nursery school or kindergarten either part- or full-time. They are experienced at playing with other children, and for the most part, they like to socialize. Unlike the younger child, the preschooler is not solely concerned with her family, though the family continues to be a strong force and an anchor for her, which is why it may be very difficult for the preschooler to move at this time.

The child who is coming into an adoptive home at this age is experiencing severe disruption of her life. In the best possible situation, she is moving out of a foster home where she has spent most or all of her previous life. She has learned to form attachments and has developed more or less along normal lines. She will experience the separation from her foster parents as a tremendous loss, akin to having them die, but coming from a situation like this, she should have enough basic stability and ego strength to be able to deal with it given time, understanding, and the consistent, loving support of her new parents.

Very few preschoolers come out of such a relatively ideal situation. Normally, when a child of this age has lived continuously with the same foster parents, they are encouraged to adopt her and may even be offered a subsidy to do that if finances would otherwise prevent the adoption. This wasn't always the case, but as the importance of attachment has been better understood, social workers and courts have become increasingly reluctant to interrupt already-established bonds. Sometimes, when the foster parents are elderly or become seriously ill, when their marriage has broken up, or occasionally, when the foster parents simply don't want to raise this child to adulthood, he or she is placed outside the foster family for adoption, but it is rarely the first choice and never easy on the child.

Most adoptable preschoolers have already experienced multiple separations and disruptions in their lives. They may have lived in several foster homes or moved back and forth between their biological families and the foster home(s). Some of them have been in group homes. These homes—we used to call them orphanages—were once quite commonplace, but since midcentury there has been a strong emphasis on placing children in families instead of institutions. Most group homes are treatment centers for children who have become so disturbed that family living doesn't work for them. In group homes, they take part in therapy and live in small familylike clusters where they gradually develop the skills for family life.

Nearly all the preschool children who are available for adoption have experienced some degree of neglect, and a great many of them have been abused or have witnessed abuse in their original families. A few of them have repeated that experience in foster homes, and some of them have already experienced rejection in a preadoptive home, or an outright adoption failure. If you are adopting a child from overseas, she may have witnessed things too horrible to remember, and she may not be in very good health. In short, the preschooler who comes to live with you may not have reached the potential she had at birth, and she will most certainly need to do some grieving and some adjusting before she begins to behave like a child her age who has had a more stable start in life.

Making the Transition

Except in an emergency, the preschooler's transition from foster home to adoptive home should be gradual. The foster parents and the social worker should tell her as soon as they know a home is available for her and, even before that, she should know that people are looking for a permanent home for her. Patterns of transition vary, but generally the adoptive parents meet their new child for the first time in a very natural setting that will not make her anxious, for example, on the playground when she is with her social worker or her foster parents, at the supermarket, or perhaps even at the foster parents' home. If there is any doubt about the placement, she will probably not be told at once that you are her adoptive parents. You will be billed as friends or acquaintances of the social worker or foster parents until the next step is assured.

The next step will likely be broaching the subject of adoption by this family with the child. The social worker is responsible for this part, but it is, in effect, a joint project. The foster family needs to reinforce what the social worker tells the child and help her deal with her fears, her feeling of rejection by the foster family, and her grief at losing them. The adoptive family may have prepared a scrapbook for the child with pictures of themselves, their other children, their house, and the room that is going to be hers. This can be an important tool in making the adoption real for her, but it needs to go hand in hand with more intense personal contact with the adoptive family.

This contact will probably take the form of an outing with the adoptive parents or a visit to their home. The temptation is to make this a very elaborate occasion, a dress-up, partylike affair, but children at this age are usually more comfortable with simple events where they can dress casually and be themselves. A picnic in the park might be more appropriate than a circus or a movie. An afternoon playing Lego would be more fun than working on an elegant and delicate dollhouse. A hot dog would probably be more of a hit than filet mignon. Children who are visiting for the first time need an activity that is familiar. It is hard enough spending time with new people. They shouldn't have to figure out how to do the activity or be expected to practice their Sunday-best manners. If the visit goes well, then another one may be planned in a few days, and after that an overnight.

An overnight is a good opportunity for parents and their new child to get to know each other in a relaxed and more or less "normal" setting. There is no great urgency to "do" something, and there are no major time constraints. The child is more likely to be herself. Both the positive and not-so-positive sides of living with her should be clearer after you have dealt with mealtime, bathing, and putting her to bed.

Your preschooler may want to call her foster parents, or she may even cry for them, especially at bedtime. It makes sense to let her set the pace for separation from them. If she needs to call them, she should be able to do that. If she is sad at being separated, she needs to hear that you understand her sadness and will support her while she deals with it. If she is miserable the first or second time she tries to stay overnight, and phoning doesn't help, there is every reason to let her go back to the foster parents to sleep and pick her up again in the morning for the rest of your time together. It is disappointing if she doesn't want to stay when you have planned it, but things need to go at a pace she can accept. When she sees that you take her needs seriously, she will be able to start trusting you. She will be able to stay overnight, even if she needs to stay in your bed all night to manage it, and she'll be able to start leaving some of her things behind in her room for the next visit.

There should be a fairly short interval between visits—just a couple of days. As soon as the child is comfortable staying overnight and being away from her foster parents for a few days at a stretch, the move to your household should be official. It needs to be quite clear where she is living and where she is visiting and the transition, while it should be at her pace, shouldn't go on forever.

If the actual move is marked in some clear way—by a small good-bye party at her foster family's house or a quiet welcome-home celebration at your home—your daughter will be better able to absorb the change. Both families should be open about the adoption being permanent so the child won't wonder when she is going back to her foster family or worry that the adoptive family will send her away. It goes without saying that this is doubly important if she has already experienced rejection or an adoption disruption.

Ideally, the preschooler should be able to maintain some contact, at least for a time, with the foster family. Attachment is such an important part of healthy emotional development that people she has been attached to should not just suddenly disappear. The interval between contacts can become longer and the contacts can be less intense; visits can be replaced by phone calls and then by notes or cards. Sometimes foster families will stay in the picture only long enough to help the child make a good transition to her adoptive parents. In other cases, it makes sense to have them involved on a longer-term basis or even permanently. The nature and length of the bond between them and your child, their relationship with you, distance, and personal preference are all going to play a part in making a decision, but the primary consideration is the welfare of your child. Whenever possible, she should have whatever she needs to help her feel that love is a stable commodity in her life.

All adopted children have a former life, even if it took place only in utero. Newly adopted preschoolers have spent their formative years with people other than the ones who become their parents. They have attachments and memories that their parents don't share. They have skills and preferences their parents had no part in forming and, for a variety of reasons, they may be hesitant to forge bonds with their new families.

When you adopt a child beyond infancy, her former life is part of the package. Her feelings about it, both positive and negative, need to be acknowledged and accepted. Her lingering affection for her foster parents, or even for biological parents who could not care for her, does not need to interfere with her attaching to you and becoming your child. Raising a child who has had a previous family (or families) is not the same as raising a child from scratch, nor should you expect it to be. It is, however, in its own unique way, a very special experience that you and your child can treasure and thrive on. But you need to be able to accept all the baggage that comes along with her.

Something All Her Own

Many children this age make their connection to the family best through siblings or extended family. They can more easily understand having new brothers and sisters, extra aunts and uncles, or a spare set of grandparents than they can understand having new parents. Parents have a unique place in their children's lives. It may take a while before your daughter can shift the old parents out of that place and adopt you for her own. Meanwhile, you can do much to make her feel she belongs.

Even before your preschooler moves in, there should be a place that is just hers—if not her own room then a bed, perhaps one you picked out together or one made up with sheets and covers of her choosing. She needs to have some space to store her belongings and those belongings—clothing, toys, books, records—should be clearly identified as hers. You may be concerned about teaching her to share, but that should wait until she feels comfortably a part of your family and believes that her things really do belong to her. Many children who have had a disrupted life in the early years cling fiercely to their material possessions as the only real security. She may not be willing to let go of that possessiveness until she is secure in your love and commitment to her.

On the other hand, some children appear to have no attachment at all to their possessions. They give them up without protest—even give them away—and may appear to be very generous. They may need some gentle encouragement to hang on to their things, to treasure them, to believe that they really are theirs to keep. They need to get to know their own boundaries and to have those boundaries respected if they are going to develop into secure people who can recognize and respect other people's boundaries.

Many children at this age, even those who have had a stable upbringing, still cling to a "luvie." It may be a blanket (usually, by this time, in the most disreputable shape), a teddy bear (loved to shreds), a pacifier, a bottle, or any of a number of imaginable or unimaginable objects. You may be tempted to replace the old blanket with one that is new (and clean) or give your child a brand-new teddy bear. At this age, you could be tempted to urge her to give up the pacifier or the bottle. Try to resist these temptations. She really needs to cling to the old while she is accommodating herself to the new.

You may, under your daughter's careful supervision, be able to clean up her luvie a bit, and you can give her a new blanket or teddy to mingle with the old ones, but don't let your concern for aesthetics interfere with her security needs. If she is going to give up her luvies, she will give them up at her own pace. If she doesn't give them up, does it really matter? The ten-year-old with an ancient teddy bear will be in good company at Brownie Scout Camp. The teenager who still sleeps with a scrap of blanket will probably get into the college of her choice, and the adult whose thumb still slips into her mouth when she is tired doesn't need to mention it on her résumé.

There may be some justifiable concern about children who sleep with bottles in their mouths. There is good evidence that they suffer serious tooth decay from the milk. But even here, you need to keep things in perspective. Teeth are easier to fix than psyches. Until your child is settled with you, don't pressure her to give up her bottle if she is very attached to it. Later, you can explain the problems for her teeth and ask her to substitute water. By this age, most children can cooperate to this extent.

Helping Her Learn the Routine

Making a visible place for your new child and the bits and pieces of her past is the first step to helping her belong. Involving her in the routines of your life and in plans for your future together is the next step. You may not think your household has much of a routine, but every family has a style that is familiar to its members and may be hard for outsiders to figure out.

Your adopted preschooler will, at first, be an outsider trying to figure you out. Help her by guiding her through the day, explaining what you have done, what you are doing now, and what is coming up next. She might appreciate a visual chart of the daily activities: eating breakfast, brushing her teeth afterward, making her bed (with lots of help at this age), going to nursery school or story hour. Don't assume she knows even the simplest routines. If you wash your hands before a meal or ask a blessing or read a story before bedtime, tell her as often as she needs to hear until she grasps the pattern of your day.

Put your daughter's birthday on the calendar—in red letters—as soon as she comes, and help her become familiar with the rituals you use to celebrate birthdays, Christmas, Easter, and the other days that are special in your family. Let her take part in the baking, the wrapping up, the decorating, and the worship that make up these special days. She will need several repetitions and explanations of why you do things the way you do before your ways come naturally to her.

The preschooler has to adapt not only to a new home and family but to many outsiders as well. Unless it is already a regular part of her life, you may want to delay sending her to nursery school or kindergarten until she gets used to things at home, but she will probably get thrust into the extended family, the neighborhood, and the church right away. Be prepared to have her sit glued to you when the grandparents want a close-up look or a hug. You may be the tallest person in the sandbox as she makes tentative steps to play with other children, and you can expect to listen to the sermon on the loudspeaker while you sit beside her in Sunday school.

If your child does go to school, you may also be a regular member of the class for a while until she feels safe in trying her wings alone. Don't be stampeded by public opinion into leaving her on her own before she is ready. She has already made more adjustments in her short life than most children, and even the most stable child sometimes wants her mother by her side when she explores the outside world. She is doing well to venture into the world with you in tow. Sooner or later, she will be ready to try it without you.

Time and Touching

The early months together are the time you are forging bonds and becoming a family. Just as you would expect to spend a lot of time with a new husband or wife or a brand-new baby, you should expect to spend a lot of time with a newly adopted child, however old she is. Time—and touching—are the magic ingredients in developing any new relationship.

If you have yearned for this child, you probably won't need much persuasion to take time with her, to encourage her to get in touch with you, to sit beside you or climb up in your lap. You'll have no trouble inventing ways to be together, to involve her in your daily life. When you let her knead the bread with you, when you read her a story, or take her around the block to try out her new training wheels, you are fulfilling your own dreams as you are building a relationship with your child.

Her initial hesitancy may be discouraging, but if you are persistent, your preschooler will begin to trust you. She will ask for her favorite story instead of passively listening to what you select; she will come to you when she falls and hurts herself. You will find her in your bed in the middle of the night when she has had a bad dream or has just gotten lonesome, and she will test your love and steadfastness by acting up a little (or a lot).

Setting Limits

Setting limits is an important part of loving your child, because you want her to be fit to live among civilized people. A lot of children have difficulty with limits; if their lives have been unstable, they are more likely than normal to have difficulty with them. As you are familiarizing your child with the routines in your house, you will automatically be filling her in on many of the limits. She may step over those limits because:

1. She didn't understand or forgot what they were.
2. The limits are very different from what she is used to.
3. She is testing you.

If you have been able to get good information from your child's foster parents or have access to them, it can be very helpful in figuring out what limits she is accustomed to and where you need to concentrate your guidance. You should also be able to find out from them how she learns best and what sort of gentle persuasions she responds to. This kind of information is not likely to be in the standard agency record, but it can be invaluable in managing any difficulties she has adapting to your limits.

Distraction and removal from the scene of temptation are still effective at this age, but more and more a child can understand—and sometimes accept—verbal explanations for your rules. Remember that slipups are inevitable for any child her age. Try to see her as an amateur person instead of a naughty or willful child.

Growing up and learning to control impulses is difficult for any child. For an insecure child whose life to date has not been stable, it is that much harder. It will get easier as she gets to know you and trust you, but before she settles down—and even afterward—she will probably do a lot of testing. She will wonder if you really mean what you say and, more important, if you will continue to love her even if she misbehaves. You can help her get through this testing phase by keeping the rules clear and simple, by being consistent, and by dealing with any acting out firmly, calmly, and gently.

At this age, it is often enough just to stop the behavior, either with a verbal reminder or by removing the child bodily from the scene. If you believe punishment would be an effective tool in helping her remember not to misbehave in this way, try to keep it brief so she will remember what it is all about. A ten-minute "time-out" in her room, or a short time of enforced boredom on a chair in an uninteresting corner of the house, is really sufficient. Long-term punishments, such as restricting television later in the day or canceling a planned-on treat, aren't effective with this age group.

Whenever possible, try to let natural consequences take care of things. For instance, if she persists in hitting a child who is visiting, the child will probably want to go home and she won't have anyone to play with. Spanking a preschooler is a risky proposition, especially if she has had any abuse in her background. What she really needs to learn is that love is powerful—more powerful than any mischief she can cook up. She probably already knows that grown-ups are more powerful than she is. Spanking is only going to reinforce her fear and distrust of adults.

Therapy Might Help

Because of their difficult backgrounds, many children who are adopted at this age profit from psychotherapy. Your child may already be working with a therapist who is helping her deal with her grief and anger over losing her original family (or families), and the scars she has gotten during her short lifetime. Therapy for children is conducted very differently from adult therapy. To the untrained eye, it might appear that the therapist is "only" playing with the child and charging a hefty fee to do it. But play therapy is a lot more than play. The therapist structures it very carefully so the child reveals her feelings and her fears as she plays with a dollhouse and its family, as she draws or paints, as she builds (and destroys) block and Lego creations. The older preschooler may grow comfortable enough in her therapist's "playroom" to talk directly about the ways she has been hurt and the fears she has, but most children of this age express themselves better indirectly.

Your child's therapist can be a wonderful help in her adjustment to your family and provide great insight into her behavior. If your child is seeing a therapist when she comes to live with you, the therapist can be an important source of stability during the transition between homes. If she is not seeing a therapist and you are finding her adjustment difficult—for both of you—consider finding a good child psychologist/psychiatrist to work with her. It is not a reflection on your parenting or your love for her—any more than calling in a doctor to treat her ear infection implies that you have not cared for her carefully enough.

Professional consultants can play an important role in many families, especially at times of great stress or transition. Your whole family can benefit from the work a therapist does with your adopted preschooler.

Eight

The
School-Age Child

The child who comes to her family when she is six or older is pretty much formed. You need to be willing to accept her, quirks and all, and realize that you will not exert as much influence as you would have had you had her from birth or early childhood. But raising her and watching her unfold can be an exciting experience nonetheless. Teachers, who have children in their classrooms for only a few hours a day and usually for only a year at a time, know how to draw children out and encourage this unfolding. Parents of school-age children have still more time with them than their teachers do, and they have them for years. If your expectations are reasonable and you are attuned to the gifts your child has already developed, you can expect to be a powerful influence in the life of your six- to twelve-year-old adopted child.

Bonding With the School-Age Child

At any age, bonding is the critical factor that makes a relationship possible—or impossible. There is actually some advantage for bonding in adopting a school-age youngster. Children in this age bracket are usually consulted about the adoption. Their initial meetings with their new families are "on approval." They don't have to accept any family that has been selected for them. Adoptable children of this age generally want to be adopted very much. They may have the same anger and grief as younger children over losing their original family (ies), but they aren't as likely to fantasize that they can recover or repair the past. They know that their route to a family is through adoption, and they are likely to come into the adoption with some commitment to making it work. You can't expect an adult-sized commitment—even from a child near the end of this age range—but for the most part, they are interested in making this new family work, even if they don't know exactly how to go about it.

The school-age child needs to be touched just as much as the younger child, perhaps even more since she may have been deprived in the past, but she may not be as open to it as a younger child. If she has experienced any sexual abuse in the past, being touched may be particularly difficult for her to tolerate. Her feelings and her pace need to be respected. If she is uncomfortable at first, go slowly. An arm around her shoulder, a quick pat on the head, a little help with brushing her hair or buttoning an out-of-reach button may be all she can stand at first. If she is young enough, she might enjoy sitting next to you or being held on your lap for a story or to watch television.

It may take quite a while before the child is comfortable with a real hug or a kiss. On the other hand, some children are so starved for affection that their needs may seem outsized and inappropriate for their age. The more thorough the background information you have from the agency and the foster parents, the better able you will be to gauge the need—and the tolerance—your child has for being touched.

Much of your bonding will take place as you share activities and talk with your child. The school-age child may express her need to be near you by "shadowing" you, by "being underfoot," by asking seemingly hundreds of questions. You can expect to spend much more time and effort with a child who is adopted at this point than you would with a child who had been living with you all along. There is a lot of catching up to do as you build your relationship, and usually a lot of making up for difficult experiences she had earlier.

If you are realistic about your child's limitations and tuned in to her emotional needs, this can be a wonderful time to adopt a child. The six- to twelve-year-old is just the right age to fit into the fantasies a lot of parents have about children. She has mastered the basic life skills that occupy the younger child, and she is ready to expand her world. This is your golden opportunity to share your interests with her. She has enough coordination to learn to ski or swim or skate; she can grasp the rules for playing baseball or soccer or tennis, and she is open to new adventure. Take her fishing or for a walk in the woods or out for a sail, and her fresh vision of the things you love will enhance your delight in them.

At home your child will probably enjoy baking bread or building something in the cellar with you and will find uses for her emerging reading and math skills. This is the peak age for game playing. You will be able to graduate from Candy Land and get into Monopoly, checkers, and chess with her.

As you work and play together, the bond between you will grow and her developing competency will help her feel better about herself. Giving her some regular responsibility such as making her bed, setting the table, and drying the dishes, will add to her sense that she is a capable and necessary member of the family (even if she grumbles about doing the work). Because her earlier life might have been quite disorderly and disruptive, she may not come to you with the skills you would expect at her age. Give her a hand until she figures out how to do the job, and make sure she understands each of the components of a job before you ask her to be responsible for it.

As she is establishing her ties to you, your child may want to hang onto the ties she had earlier. If she has been in a foster home, she may want to stay in contact with her foster parents and the other children who lived there. There may be brothers and sisters or other relatives from her biological family who are close to her and want to maintain contact. There are no hard and fast rules, but you should think carefully before assuming that your child will leave behind everyone who has been dear to her when she becomes a part of your family.

Supporting the relationships that have sustained the youngster in the past may well be crucial to the success of your adoption. You will probably want to explore this issue with your social worker and with your child if she is old enough, even before she comes to live with you. Find out who is important to her and work out some tentative arrangements for staying in touch. You will also want to find out who she doesn't want to see and which relationships might be a problem to her and to you. You need to be very cautious about cutting any ties that are important to her, but you also want to ensure that you can develop your own ties without unnecessary disturbances.

Your top priority is providing a stable, loving environment in which your child can thrive. Sometimes that is going to mean including people who were part of her life before you were; at other times it is going to mean excluding them. With a child of this age, the decision is largely yours, but it needs to be made carefully, prayerfully, on an individual basis.

A Change in Friends and School

In the six- to twelve-year age bracket, the child's focus is beginning to shift a little away from her home and family. Her friends and her school will be increasingly important in her life. Being adopted might mean changing schools and making new friends, and that can be almost as hard for her as changing families—but you can make it easier. Perhaps the adoption can be timed to avoid a school change in the middle of the year. If your approval comes through in May and your child has only a few weeks to finish up in her school, it makes sense to keep her where she is until school is out, all things being equal. Of course, they are never equal. There may be other concerns. Her foster family may not be able to continue caring for her. She might not be happy in school and would welcome the move, or she might simply want to have her own family regardless of the changes it means. What makes sense for one child might be disaster for another.

If your daughter is going to be changing schools, people at her old school might make the transition easier by putting together a book of pictures and writing that will remind her of her friends. An older child might want to bring an autograph book into school, and a party is always in order. Try to talk to the foster parents and her classroom teacher about easing her move, and see if you can find out from them the areas that might cause her difficulty when she does move. Encourage her to collect addresses of her friends and promise her some help in staying in touch by letter or by phone.

You can ease your child's transition at your end by meeting with her new classroom teacher, by familiarizing yourself with the curriculum and the books she will be using, and by sharing what you have learned with her in your preadoption meetings. If you can arrange for her to visit her new school before she actually has to enroll, it won't seem so strange and scary to her.

While you should be honest with school officials about any difficulties you expect her to have adjusting to a new school, you needn't paint the picture in such dark colors that they will anticipate problems with a capital P. Just remind them of what they know already: that being adopted, moving into a new family, a new school, and a new peer group is a big adjustment for any child. Let them know that your child is fundamentally sound, that you don't expect any long-lasting difficulties, and that you are available to help them help her whenever necessary.

School personnel will take their cue from you. If you prepare them for an essentially normal child who is making a stressful change, they are likely to treat her appropriately. If you overstress the difficulties she may have, they might brace themselves for a tough time, and they will probably find it.

Of course, if your child does have serious problems—learning disabilities or behavioral problems, for instance—teachers should know that so they can have the appropriate help available. Once the child is in school, monitor her homework, check fairly frequently with her teacher, and listen attentively as your child talks about her experience there to ensure that she does, in fact, get integrated smoothly into the life of her new school.

Making friends is going to be a top priority for your school-age child. Even if she is able to stay in touch by letter or phone or occasional visits with her old friends, she needs to have friends nearby. Many of those friends will be made at school, though at first it may be hard for her to find a place to fit in. You won't be able to make friends for her, but you can be a good source of support and tactful advice.

Children in this age bracket want more than anything else to be just like other children, and one of the ways they can tell if they are is by what they are wearing. If you have visited your child's classroom ahead of time, take note of what the other children are wearing and let her dress accordingly. Dress in some schools is very casual. In other schools it is quite formal. Skirts and dresses may be "in" at one school and "out" at another. Everything from hairstyle to footgear is important at this stage (and it gets even more important later on). Try—within reason—to help her fit in. You don't have to go along with every change of fashion. It is reasonable to buy her a few outfits that you both agree are satisfactory, then expect those clothes to be worn until she needs new ones—even if fashion changes midstream. You don't have to agree to outrageous hairdos or makeup or clothing that is downright sloppy or immodest, but if she can dress in a way that won't make her stand out in her class, she is going to be much more comfortable.

Find out the classroom rituals children want to be a part of. Do they come to school in costume on Halloween? Do they bring in a "grab" or a present for the teacher at Christmas? Are birthdays celebrated with a treat from home? If you like to bake, volunteer for the cookie detail when the class is having a party. If you have a special skill you would enjoy sharing or teaching to your child's class, try to arrange to come in soon after your child has joined the class—or even before. If you have something to offer that her class can appreciate, some of their good feeling about you will rub off on her.

If you don't have a talent that would interest this age level, don't worry about it. Your child is going to have to make friends mostly on her own merits. You can help her fit in a little and stay open to support the friendships she makes, but no parent can successfully orchestrate a child's friendships, nor should we try.

Once your child has made some friends, encourage her to bring them home. If your home is a warm, inviting environment, you don't have to do much more than provide snacks and supervision. You can, from time to time, include her friends on a trip to the movies or a concert. You will certainly let her have her good friends overnight and arrange for a birthday party, but most of what happens between friends is casual. Friendships can be a real antidote to too much organized activity. As long as you keep an eye on things to avoid any unnecessary bullying or mischief making, you can leave most of the decisions about what to do to your child and her friends. Get to know the parents of her friends too, so you will be comfortable letting her play away from home.

One problem that parents today have, more than their parents did, is coping with widely varying value systems. Many children are less well supervised than they need to be and are allowed to see movies and television programs you may think are inappropriate for your children.

One reason for getting to know the parents of your children's friends, apart from the obvious goal of having friendly relationships between the families, is to find out what kind of environment your child will be in when she is visiting. You can make some fairly firm rules. For instance, children between six and twelve should be supervised pretty much all the time. If you think your child will not be supervised at her friend's house, you can simply tell her—and the friend's mother—that you don't let your children go visiting when there is no parent at home, and extend an invitation to have the friend come to your house. It gets trickier if the parent is home and allows things you aren't comfortable with. You will need to figure out where to make compromises and where to stand firm.

You could probably safely agree to a visit even if you knew the children would be watching cartoons all afternoon; you would want to veto it if you knew the family had rented an R-rated movie for their VCR. When you do have to veto a visit, tact will go a long way in taking out the sting. Let your child—and her friend—know that you are vetoing the activity, not the friend or her family. Suggest that an alternative activity would make a difference in your decision, and always keep open the option of having the friend visit at your house instead.

Only very occasionally will your child make a friend whose influence on her is totally negative or whose home you would not be comfortable having her visit under any circumstances. If this happens, you need to protect her by standing firm and offering some alternative activities where she can make more suitable friends. But in most cases, it makes more sense to offer supervision for her friendships rather than to forbid them outright. If her friend is someone she knows from school or a regular activity, it is going to be impossible to keep them apart anyway, and trying to will only make the friendship seem more attractive.

Extracurricular Activities

The age range between six and twelve is a peak time for organized group activities: Scouts and Camp Fire Girls, Boys' and Girls' Clubs, youth groups, team sports, and lessons of all sorts are available in nearly every community. Encourage your child to try some of these activities on for size; a couple at a time is enough. Too much scheduling makes a child feel just as overwhelmed as it makes us feel. She needs some time when she has nothing in particular to do, when she can go read a book or lie outside and look at the clouds or do something spontaneously. She may need some help in balancing group activity and solitude. Most children will try out a number of activities before they find the ones that fit right. Because these activities are "extra" and are supposed to be fun, parents are often in a quandary if their children want to quit something they have started. We want our children to learn to stick with things, but we also want them to take pleasure in the things they do.

Usually, it is a good idea to talk things over with your child ahead of time, explaining that she may want to try out several activities and discussing the importance of making some sort of commitment to each activity she tries. Generally, it is not too much to ask your child to finish out a session, a season, or a semester when she has signed up for something (especially if you have to pay for it), but you need to be flexible. If she realizes after the first time or two that she absolutely hates whatever it is she is doing, then she is not likely to suffer any damage to her character if you let her stop right away. If, after a little more time, she is totally miserable in whatever she is doing, talk to her instructor/leader to see what is going on. She may be undergoing some intense teasing from some of the other children or she may feel she is not competent or that the leader is not sympathetic to her. Very often things can be worked out if the problem is brought to the adult leader's attention.

If the problem seems insoluble and your child is showing signs of real suffering, if she is crying before she goes and when she comes home, if she is having nightmares or her whole demeanor changes on the day her activity is scheduled, there is no point in making her finish the program. She can learn from this that we don't always know ahead of time what an experience is going to be like, that children and adults can make misjudgments, and that we are not totally powerless to change things that make us miserable. Reassure her that not all group experiences are like the one she had, and encourage her to find another activity she can do with other people fairly soon. Generally, group activities work out well at this age. It is not always true that children who take part in constructive activities make suitable friends, but more often than not that is the case. If your child and her friends have something in common, the friendships are likely to be stronger and longer lasting.

Testing . . . One, Two, Three

At this age, expect your child to do quite a lot of testing, fairly soon after she comes to live with you. A child who is available for adoption at this age has had a lot of disappointments in her relationships with other people. She is going to want to make sure that you don't disappoint her too. Making sure often involves revealing the least attractive parts of her personality to see if you will continue to love her and stay committed to her.

If you are prepared for this kind of negative behavior from your child, you are less likely to overreact with anger or fear that she is headed for no good. You need to set limits on how she can behave and she needs you to set those limits, but she also needs to be reassured that you understand why she is behaving as she is, that you don't see her misbehavior as a personal attack on you, and that she can count on your commitment to her. If her previous experience with limit setting has involved abusive behavior, she will understandably be quite anxious if you scold her or restrict her activities. She may even be defiant as a way of containing her fear.

Try to keep your eye on the goal; put an end to the behavior that was originally at issue, and avoid getting locked into an escalating battle over your daughter's attitude. Faith may, in fact, move mountains—and change behavior—but it doesn't usually happen all at once.

There is, in Christian circles, considerable controversy over physical punishment. Christians who practice nonviolence are opposed to it; Christians of the "spare the rod" school advocate it. Very few parents have never spanked a child, whatever their principles. Spanking, in any case, should not be the chastisement of choice for routine infractions. Routine spanking teaches children more about power than about respect and obedience. If your child has had a history of abuse, you should probably avoid spanking altogether. The nuances between spanking and "slapping around" are too sophisticated for most children to pick up.

Could a Therapist Help?

If your child is having serious difficulties or seems to be having an extra hard time adjusting, consider getting her into therapy. You will want to find a good play therapist for most children in this age bracket. Children toward the end of this age range can talk more about how they are feeling, but much of what goes on in therapy will take place in the context of play. Younger children reveal themselves through puppets or dollhouse play; older ones may talk more easily over a game of checkers; both groups may be open to expressing themselves by drawing or through music or dance. The guidelines in chapter 9 for finding a therapist are applicable at any age level. The younger the child, the more the therapist needs to involve the parents.

Keep in mind that the role of the therapist is to help your child learn to live more comfortably with herself and with you. The therapist should be able to interpret your child's behavior to you, to help your child make herself known to you, and to support the standards and goals in your family. She may have useful insights about your family dynamics, but she should not be attempting a major overhaul of your family. Shop around, interview carefully, and listen to your instincts before you settle on someone to work with your child. While you want to be cautious, don't hold back on getting therapy for your child if you think she needs it because of embarrassment or a previous bad experience. Many children and their parents benefit greatly from therapy. There are competent, compassionate therapists to be found, but like any worthwhile project, it takes time and effort.

Nine

Adopting a Teenager: Take One Day at a Time

Adopting a teenager is, in some ways, more like getting married than having a child. Your child is already nearly grown; she has lived much of her life without you, and your relationship is by mutual agreement. But the analogy only goes so far. The adoption of a teenager is not a partnership of two fully qualified adults. The teenager who wants to be adopted really needs parents, and the parents have to be real adults to cope with the wide range of behavior their teenager is likely to try out. In some ways, your new teenager may seem very grown up indeed and, given the sorts of life experiences that lead to a teenager's being available for adoption, that should not be surprising. But in other ways she may be quite a bit younger than you expected—and that should be no surprise either. An adoptable teenager has usually missed out on a great deal of her childhood and on the kind of parenting she needs to grow up.

Talk Over Your Expectations

Even if your son or daughter is not adopted or was adopted as an infant, there are rough times during the teenage years. That goes with the territory, but the teenager who has had no stable home or has experienced a disruption of her family life is even more likely to present a serious challenge to her family. Unrealistic expectations—on both sides—are the most common source of friction in families that have adopted teenagers. Some of this friction can be prevented by talking about your expectations before the adoption, but much of it is going to have to be worked out on a day-to-day basis.

Very often the family and the teenager are so eager for the adoption to take place that they don't discuss their expectations very thoroughly, or they convince themselves that love will be enough to deal with all the problems that come up. That is no truer in adoption than it is in marriage, but the partners to both kinds of family making regularly act as though it were, and just as regularly suffer from their lack of foresight and planning.

The early weeks after the adoption may be a sort of honeymoon period during which the teenager and her parents are on their best behavior. The parents marvel at how "good" she is and bend over backward to please her. Their teenager keeps up a good front too, but her experience has been that people disappoint her and, sooner or later, she is going to test her new parents with behavior that may upset and shock them. The biggest mistake parents can make at this point is to overreact. Especially if they already have had teenagers they raised from early childhood, they may have expectations for their teen's behavior that she can't possibly meet or that she will meet only very gradually.

If you are planning to adopt a teenager, try to get a very complete idea of her background. Ask for medical and psychiatric records, talk with social workers, teachers, and therapists who know her well, and try to understand the stresses and the losses that have shaped her life. You can virtually guarantee that a teenager available for adoption will be troubled in some way. Find out what problems the teen you are interested in has, and be honest about your ability to cope with them. You are not in the business of rescuing but of family making. Wait until you have done all the legwork before you arrange a personal meeting. That way you don't get hopes up unnecessarily.

Your prospective teenager might ask for some information about you and your family before she agrees to meet with you. Be glad she is so cautious. It indicates that she wants the adoption to work out too. Many families like to prepare a collection of photos and letters describing their family for social workers to share. This sort of introduction to your family could be a big help to your teenager, not only as she is making up her mind whether or not to meet you but also, once the decision is made, to help your family seem familiar even before you have met.

The introduction of a teenager into the family is generally a slow process. First there may be a meeting or two at the agency to help both the teenager and her prospective family find out if they would, in fact, like to try to become a family. She may go with the family for an outing or a weekend; they may visit her in her foster home or the residential center where she lives. If the brief visits go well, she can move in with her new family. That move may be quite gradual, especially if her present home is nearby. As she changes homes, she may also have to change schools and make new friends. It can be quite overwhelming at an age when school and friends have the most prominent place in her life. Understandably, she may be reluctant to sever her old ties and, as much as feasible, she should be allowed to stay in touch with people who were close to her before her adoption.

How the Past Affects Your Teenager

Your child's past is going to have a tremendous impact on her current life and on yours. This is why it is important to know as much about it as possible and to understand how to deal with some of the fallout. The most fundamental concerns in your household are going to be affected by it.

Bonding will probably be a primary concern. Bonding requires some ability to trust, and an adoptable teenager has almost always had that capacity damaged to some degree. If she has been in therapy and a stable placement for a while, she may have healed enough to try out trusting, but there will be a lot of testing before she is sure she has found reliable people.

Touch, the kind of body language you use almost without thinking to establish a bond with a younger child, needs to be used with discretion with teenagers. In part this has to do with her age and the need of all teenagers to have their boundaries respected. A teenager may reject all physical signs of affection as "childish," or she may have grown up in a household where people did not touch or where affectionate displays were a way of getting things ("Give Mommy a kiss and I'll let you go to the movies"). If she has been sexually abused, she may be extremely wary about being touched. Be respectful of her boundaries, but let her see that affection is a normal part of your household. Once she realizes that affectionate touch is genuine —and safe—in your household, she may be more open to it.

The past will affect your teenager's behavior in other ways too. She may come to you with habits you find objectionable: vulgar language, smoking, certain hairstyles and ways of dress, behavior which is not in itself "bad" but which offends other people (bad table manners, playing the stereo at top volume, poor attention to grooming). These are behaviors that any teenager can have, but if you have raised a child all or most of her life, she will know what your standards are and she is not likely to have a large collection of objectionable behaviors.

105

Your newly adopted teen may not even realize that some of her behaviors are objectionable and may be surprised—even angry—when you speak to her about them. If you have learned a lot about her before you meet her, you will be prepared for these behaviors and you will have had a chance to decide which ones are real priorities to work on and which ones can be left alone. If you try to change too much at once, you are asking for trouble. Some of what your teenager does is testing, but she genuinely needs to feel accepted more or less as she is. If she feels that acceptance, she will be more open to accommodating you with some changes. If, on the other hand, she feels that you are doing nothing but criticizing her, she is going to have a harder time wanting to make these changes—and may even give up.

Setting Behavior Standards

If you have other children at home, you can count on some flak from them if you let your new child get away with things that they are not allowed to do. You may forestall some of the murmurings among your troops by sitting down with them before your new teenager arrives for a discussion about the behavior standards that are important in your family. If your children are committed to at least some of the standards, it will be easier to enlist their help in guiding your new child. Your other children may, in fact, be the best teachers of all because at this age the opinions of peers (and brothers and sisters fall into the peer category) are much more important in shaping behavior than the opinions of parents or other adults.

You will have to set limits, but save those limits for the really important things—and don't overwhelm your new teenager with lists of rules. Your other children have learned the rules gradually, over a period of years. It is not so overwhelming to learn that way. This child needs to have some time to learn your rules and adapt herself to them, and you'll need a lot of tact and patience as you wait for her to learn them.

Some sorts of behavior need to be dealt with at once because they are so risky for your teen. Drugs, alcohol, and sexual acting out fall into this category. The sad truth is that children from all sorts of families do a lot of experimenting with these things, but children who have had a troubled family life or emotional crises are even more likely to use drugs and sex to blot out the pain—and even when things begin to improve, they may have a hard time stopping these habits. Hopefully your preplacement research will have given you some indications as to whether these areas are a problem for your teenager. If they are, she needs to be in therapy, and the family will need some supportive therapy as well to help them cope.

Especially in the area of chemical abuse and dependence, there is a considerable spread of opinion about appropriate treatment, but among professionals with training in psychology or psychiatry, there is fairly widespread agreement that chemical abuse usually does not develop in a vacuum.

Dr. Sandra Eisemann, a psychologist working with children, adolescents, and their families in Madison, Wisconsin, notes: "In a substantial number of cases, the teenager who abuses drugs or alcohol is depressed and is, in effect, medicating herself." She and her colleagues encourage their young patients *not* to use drugs and alcohol, but "we need to find out what is making our patients feel so bad that they use drugs to make themselves feel better. If we treat the underlying causes, they have a better chance of being able to stop the drugs or alcohol." If your teenager is not already in therapy with someone she—and you—can trust, find someone else. It is perfectly acceptable to interview prospective therapists to find a good match. Fundamentally what you are looking for is a therapist who has the following qualifications:

- *Good credentials:* a master's or doctor's degree in psychology, counseling, social work, or, in some cases, psychiatry.
- *A respectful attitude* toward your teenager, toward you as her parents, and toward the sort of family life you have. It would be ideal to have a Christian therapist, but a non-Christian who re-

spects the position faith has in your family life and makes an effort to understand your beliefs and values will do far more good than a Christian who is inadequately trained.

- *A willingness to work in partnership with your family,* an openness to your questions, comments, and suggestions, and the humility to seek a consultation if she—or you—think a second head would be useful.
- *That indefinable thing we call "chemistry"* that tells us right off we can work together. You and your child are going to be sharing your most intimate thoughts, hopes, and sometimes despair with the therapist. It is not too much to ask that you like each other.

There are, in some Christian circles, strong objections to therapy. Love and prayer, it is believed, should be enough to carry any family, no matter how troubled. But there is another point of view. God works through the people and things we encounter in life. Just as He often works through physicians to cure physical illnesses, so does He work through mental health practitioners to heal broken spirits and damaged psyches. The spontaneous or instant healing is the exception—whether the illness is physical or emotional. God heals miraculously from time to time, when for His purposes He wants to attract our attention, but mostly He works more quietly through the hands of the practitioners and physicians we select. Prayer is still vital to hold up these healers and their patients, but in most cases God expects us not only to call upon Him but also to use the resources He has placed at hand for us.

Family Activities

While most teenagers who are available for adoption do come from troubled backgrounds and have painful issues to deal with, most are quite capable of living in a family and contributing positively to it. They may need some supports, like therapy or ongoing contact with people who have been helpful to them in the past, but if they are going to live in a family, they want to be a real part of it. It is tempting at first to treat a new child like a guest, but that simply slows her integration into the family. She needs to know the important rules of the family and have a clear idea of what your expectations are.

Like the other children, your daughter needs to be assigned chores, be given an allowance (or a chance to earn it), and share in all the things you do together. Not all the learning she needs to do will be tedious. If your family plays Monopoly or Scrabble together, if you ski or sail, you may need to teach her some new skills so she can take part. Very early on you will want to introduce her to the extended family, get her into family pictures, and acquaint her with family history, shared jokes, and your favorite haunts. She becomes a part of your family with this sort of sharing, and you become a part of hers when she shares her history and skills and special places with you. Some families make a point of learning something new together, working on a joint project or going somewhere none of them have been before, soon after their new teenager moves in. There are probably as many family-building activities as there are families to think them up. The point is that families don't just happen—especially when you are adopting a teenager. You need to make an effort to grow together.

Outside Interests Are Important

As much as your teenager has wanted a family, she is also going to want to be involved outside the family. Peers are very important to any teenager's life and, for the teenager who has not had a stable family before, peers may play a more central role. Your other children will be a vital part of that peer group and their friends will extend it for her, but she will want to choose friends of her own as well.

Most friendships are made at school because most teenagers spend a large number of their waking hours there, but your daughter may also make friends in the neighborhood and in the places where teenagers gather to socialize. Many parents are concerned—and rightly so—that their children will make inappropriate friendships if they just "hang out." Most teenagers will do a certain amount of "hanging out," but it is smart to get them involved in constructive activities as much as possible. Team sports are one possibility; Sunday school and youth groups are another. Your teenager might enjoy joining the "Y" or the Boys' (Girls') Club to swim or sail or work out. She might enjoy learning to play an instrument or, if she plays one, she might want to play in a group. It is all right to encourage her to take part in activities that are wholesome.

Unless she has grown up in your community, your teenager probably will need—and welcome—your guidance about the activities available to her. It is also all right to designate some activities—Sunday school and youth group, for instance—as nonoptional, but it is important to strike a balance so your guidance doesn't become coercion (nor should you abandon her to her own devices in your eagerness to encourage her to make independent decisions).

Welcome your teenager's friends into your home—even if their hair is a little long, their clothes a little sloppy (or more than a little), or their values are a little at variance with your own. You certainly want to point out tactfully where there are enormous differences in values or beliefs, but your daughter is going to encounter all sorts of people and as long as she wants to bring them home, and they feel welcomed by you, her friends are not likely to exert a very bad influence on her. Make a special effort to accommodate her friends from the past—or any of her brothers or sisters, if possible. She is part of your family, but she has brought the past with her, and that past needs to be accepted graciously.

Adopting a teenager is not the easiest project in the world to undertake. There are lots of built-in difficulties, but there are bonuses too. When you adopt a teenager, you are getting a nearly grown young person. If she is not yet a fully qualified adult, she is very nearly there, she is probably committed to making the adoption work and can anticipate what she needs to do to make it work. The fruits of your labors with teenagers are apparent very quickly, and you have the benefits of the blossoming she has already done. Teenagers carry on good conversations and can share in the things you enjoy—and they usually have plenty to teach as well. The adoption of a teenager is not the usual way to build a family, but with realistic expectations and a willingness to work, it can be a very satisfying way to start or expand a family.

Ten

Your Child Grows Up

Eventually, every child grows up and the concerns of child-hood seem very distant. You have forged a bond with your child, had the pleasure (and the pain) of raising her, and now she is off on her own. But this is hardly the end of parent-hood in most families. Relating to adult children is a whole new phase which may last far longer than the active child rearing did. Adulthood means a loosening of the bonds built by day-to-day living together. Shared history and affection are the foundation stones for new adult-to-adult ties. If you live close by, these bonds can continue to thrive on frequent contact. If you don't—and twentieth-century families tend to be spread out fairly widely—you will have to rely on letters, the telephone, and sporadic visits to maintain your relationship with your adult children.

How Much Contact?

Because families so easily drift apart under the pressures of daily living and distance, it makes good sense to sit down with your children before they leave home and talk about the sort of relationship and contact you all want to have with one another. Some families decide on a weekly letter written the same day each week; other families schedule phone calls at regular intervals. Large families often like round-robin letters passed from one member of the family to the next (participants in this sort of project need to be very dependable letter writers if the system is going to work).

While we sometimes complain about the number of special occasions the greeting-card industry has invented to get our business, the wide variety of cards available is just what the far-flung family needs. We might not bother with cards as long as we are together to share special days, but a well-chosen card can light up your child's day, not only on Valentine's Day and Easter and birthdays, but also on the days she is feeling under the weather, when she has exams or an important job interview—or for no reason at all. Flowers, balloons, and exam-time first-aid kits (with nuts and fruits and other things to nibble instead of her fingernails) are all ways of staying in touch, of saying "I love you"—even when you are far away.

A certain amount of distance is normal and necessary for the adult child to grow up and build her own life. When she first leaves home, she may create some of that distance with irritability or adoption of a life-style that makes you uncomfortable. Relations may be quite strained during this time, but generally it lasts only a couple of years. No parent is really prepared for the distancing, but adoptive parents may be especially vulnerable to believing that they—or the adoption—are somehow responsible for the cooling of their relationship with their child. If she chooses this time to embark on a search for her biological family, it may be even harder to see this as a neutral stage in her growing-up process. Like any other stage, this one is the hardest with a first (or only) child. With subsequent children you will normally have had a chance to see an earlier child come through it and reestablish her relationship with you on an adult basis, and you will have more perspective when this stage reappears in your next child.

While you probably should not let yourself be thrown by some irritability and distance, open, ongoing hostilities or a total lack of communication between you and your adult child should be of concern. Very often you will have seen signs of this earlier. The distancing and testing you expect in a teenager may have been quite extreme. If you have seen it soon enough, you may have been able to get your child and the family into therapy. But sometimes the signs don't show up early or you haven't considered therapy or your child has not been open to it. She may leave your home quite determined not to come back. There is not much you can do to force an adult child to maintain ties with her family, but there are things you can do to prevent her departure from devastating you—and the rest of the family—and to leave the door open to a relationship later on down the road.

All parents need to keep in mind that their lives cannot totally revolve around their children. Right from the start, parents are going to need other relationships and interests to give them balance and to prevent smothering. Children *are* important, absorbing, and require lots of time and attention, but parents do the whole family a favor by having some life of their own—even if it needs to be squeezed into the odd moments during the busy years. Parents with their own interests will be better able to weather the storms in their relationships with their children, even such a major storm as an angry departure at the end of adolescence.

If your child's departure *is* angry, there is no point in creating a scene of your own or in tracking her down obsessively, but you can let her know verbally, in writing, or in your communications with people who are in touch with her that she could call, write, or visit without fear of rejection from you.

Parents need to realize that there are no guarantees in the child-rearing business. The choice to have and adopt children is ours. In most cases, the children had little or nothing to say about it. We have hopes and plans for them and for our families as a whole. Some of those dreams are fulfilled; some are not. When our dreams do come true—and when they don't—it is all too easy to take the credit (or blame) for it, but we are not the only factor.

Our children are individuals who make decisions on their own. There are often circumstances outside our families that influence what goes on within the family. Overseeing it all is God's Providence. We have grand designs, but if they are in conflict with God's plans for us, we may find our lives inexplicably veering off in directions we had not foreseen. This is not to say that we can't take some credit for our successes. After all, they do involve a lot of dedication and hard work on our part. Nor does it mean we can't take some blame when things go wrong. We do fall short of what we should—and could—do, and quite often there are consequences to pay. What we do need to do is keep things in perspective. We are never totally responsible for what other people do, nor does a relationship rest solely on one person.

If your relationship with your adult child is troubled, you may need to be patient. Look to your own behavior to see if it is creating some barrier to being on good terms with your child, but don't feel that you need to accept any sort of behavior from her just to keep in contact with her. Adult relationships are built on mutual affection and respect. You don't do your child or your family a favor to tolerate behavior that would be unacceptable in any other relationship. Let her know what the limits are, remind her that your door is always open if she is open to an adult relationship with you, then let her go. You can keep the door open, even when there is great alienation, with prayer, occasional cards and notes, and by being discreet as you share with others the troubles you have with her. When there has been some tie of respect and affection in the past, most of these strained relationships can be healed in time.

Searching for Roots

Relationships in adoptive families are sometimes strained when the adoptee wants to search for her original family. Many adoptive parents feel wounded and betrayed when their child searches, or even talks about, the possibility. It doesn't have to be a source of friction. Most adoptees who search are not dissatisfied with their adoptive families. They are not looking for their "real" parents but rather for themselves. In a root-conscious society, adoptees are the only group of adults who don't know about their personal and biological histories. They usually don't have anything approaching a complete medical background, and if that background should prove vital to their health, they may not be able to get access to it. Imagine not knowing where that red hair came from, if your grandfather was bald—or diabetic—whether your ancestors came over on the Mayflower or in the steerage section of a nineteenth-century ship. Imagine not knowing whether you are Scottish, Italian, or Lithuanian in background, and imagine never having known anyone to whom you have blood ties.

Most of us take for granted our fairly extensive knowledge of our origins, and we pass that information along to our children. But history, ancestors, and blood ties can't be passed along by adoption. Many adoptees feel a great need to acquire histories of their own. Part of that process may be searching for biological parents, but the vast majority of adoptees have no intentions or illusions about replacing the parents who raised them with the people who gave them life.

The best thing you can do for your child if she wants to search is to help her. Let her know you support her and you understand why she wants to find out more about her background. If you really do feel threatened by her desire to search, let her know you feel that way, but make it clear to her that you know it is your problem and you are working on it—then really do work on it.

You may be able to give your daughter more than moral support. You might have some practical leads that will facilitate her search. Adoption practices vary widely from state to state. While some parents have very scanty records, others have quite complete information. Share what you have with her and offer to go back to the adoption agency with her if she would like. Sometimes agencies are more open to sharing information if the adoptee has the support of her adoptive family.

Even the information the agency shares may not be enough for your child to make much headway in her search. If she is not satisfied with the information she is able to get through this route, encourage her to contact an adoption search group. Both birthparents and adoptees may register with these groups, and a number of them have found one another when the computer made a match.

When there is no instant computer match, these groups have an assortment of procedures for gathering information that can be helpful. Records are very rarely destroyed or actually "sealed." They are simply made "off limits" to the parties concerned with the adoption. If the records can be accessed—and more often than not they can—the information is there for the reading. What your adult child is likely to find in the records is the name, address, and birth date of her birthmother, and sometimes the birthfather as well.

This information won't necessarily lead your daughter straight to her birthfamily. It may be twenty years or more out of date, but it is a start and may be the first "hard" data she has. From there, depending on how much information she has and how out of date it is, her search could take a few minutes or a few years.

Whether the search is short or long, you can expect that it will cause some anxiety for all of you, and once the birthfamily has been located, the anxiety level will go up. While you are worrying about whether your adult child will prefer the birthfamily to yours, she is worrying about what she will find, about being disappointed, and about being rejected. You can't easily reassure her about these things, but you can reassure her that whatever she finds and whatever reception she gets, you will continue to be her parents and to find her quite acceptable.

Most adoptees want to make their initial contacts with their birthfamily alone. If you have helped her in her search, you may feel a little left out if she wants to proceed on her own, but this is a time when she needs for you to let go and let her go forward alone. If you have supported her to this point, she will share her experience with you in her own time. If things go well, she will probably want you to meet her biological family eventually—and then you may find yourself adding a whole new branch to your family tree.

Take your cue from your child. Some adoptees prefer to keep their two families separate—at least for a time. In some cases, the situation in either the birthfamily or the adoptive family prevents the families from getting together. Try to be open to what suits your child. Your relationship will be the better for it if you don't force her to feel uncomfortable about her choice. If she is disappointed or rejected in her search, she is going to need the support you promised her. She may feel bad about herself for a while. You can reassure her that she is loved and lovable, and remind her that she searched not only to find her birthfamily but also to find herself. Whatever she has discovered or experienced, she has come to know herself better and to understand the circumstances that brought her into your home. Once she has had a chance to absorb what she has learned—positive or negative—she will probably be even closer to you than she was before, if you have supported her in her search.

The Never-Empty Nest

Distance is the issue that most concerns parents when they think about their children growing up, but the issue that many families deal with in actuality is adult children who don't separate, who come back to live at home after they have left or come back to be rescued when they are in trouble. Adult children who are too dependent on their parents are just as worrisome as the ones who are too distant.

What is "too dependent"? We want to be available to help our children and other people in our families when that help is really needed. Few families want to pack their children off forever the day they turn eighteen; fewer still will turn them away when they are in real need, but it is important to set some limits. The kind of limits will depend on your family's style and background and the needs the individual members of your family have.

If your family has experienced multigenerational living comfortably in the past, you will probably be more open to having your adult children live with you before they go out on their own. You will have different expectations of the "right" age for them to leave and of their responsibilities to you, than another family might.

What is important is that your adult children behave like adults and carry adult responsibilities, however you define them. An adult child who is working, living at home, and not contributing financially and practically is not behaving like an adult. The mother who races home after her full-time job to make supper for an adult child who gets home an hour ahead of her is not letting her child be an adult.

Sometimes parents are reluctant to ask their children to take on adult responsibilities because they don't want to alienate them, or simply because they aren't yet ready to let their children grow up. That is a disservice to the whole family. The resentments that build up cause more damage than any open discussion of changing rules could ever do.

The adult who returns in crisis is a slightly different story. People in crisis rarely have the emotional wherewithal to act like adults all the time. Offering your adult child a place of retreat and sanctuary when she is in crisis is entirely appropriate. As things settle down and she is feeling better, she will probably want to pick up her responsibilities again. By definition, a crisis is short-lived. Supporting her through it, if your own life is reasonably stable, is not likely to put undue strain on your resources or your relationship.

Dealing With Conflicts

What does strain relationships is coping with an adult child who has chosen a life-style or values that are in conflict with yours. These value conflicts may be relatively simple; for example, she may smoke or use alcohol socially. These conflicts can be handled relatively easily by respecting each other's rules when you are not on your own turf.

More serious conflicts call for careful thought, patience, and tact. If she is living with her boyfriend and you don't approve of that, if she has stopped going to church or has joined a cult, the conflict between you may not be so easily resolved. Maintaining a relationship without condoning behavior you don't approve of is tricky. If your communication has been pretty good all along, it will be easier to tell her how uncomfortable you are with her behavior without making her feel rejected. If your communication has not been good, you will need a double dose of tact to share your concerns without alienating her entirely.

Once you have shared your concerns, there is no need to keep at it. Your children know your values and they know when their values are in conflict with yours. They will appreciate your honesty with them if you mix it thoroughly with affection for them and respect for their boundaries. Unsolicited preaching is not a very effective tool for change. Patience and prayer for your child and for yourself are more likely to bring about changes.

Sometimes conflicts signal that your child is in deep personal trouble. She may have trouble with drugs or alcohol, she may have some legal difficulties, or she may be suffering from some sort of emotional illness. No amount of tact or patience will solve these problems. Taking a firm stand against the behavior and insisting on some sort of intervention is the most constructive way you can deal with problems of this magnitude. If she is open (even under some pressure) to getting some help, your support will be invaluable; if she is not (and, if she is competent to make that decision), then you may have to let go with prayer and a promise of an open door when she is ready to be helped.

When our children are young, it is tempting to believe they belong to us. Adoptive parents may develop an even stronger proprietary sense than other parents because there is competition, usually unrecognized and not discussed, somewhere in the background. The teen and young adult years gradually disabuse us of this fantasy that we own our children, but we may suffer all the fear, jealousy, and panic that goes with possessive love before we realize no one can truly belong to anyone else. Only when that is clear will we be free to build relationships with our children that are based on mutual affection, trust, and respect. Only then can we have some assurance that the family we have so carefully nurtured and cherished will continue to be vital and life-giving for us all.

Eleven

Forming Other Relationships

When we think of bonding, we are usually thinking about the tie between parent and child, but children have ties to all sorts of people besides their parents and these need to be nurtured carefully too. If your child has had a history of relationships that have fallen apart or ended inexplicably, she will be very cautious about establishing new ties and may need a lot of help in learning how to trust and how to conduct herself.

After the "Honeymoon"

If you have other children, your new child will have an immediate immersion course in sibling relationships. At first all the children are likely to be on their best behavior. A new brother or sister is a pretty exciting event, and having one close enough in age to be an instant playmate looks like a pretty good arrangement. The children you already have may outdo themselves to be kind and generous; your new child will probably revel in all the attention and transitory glory. But don't get too complacent.

Just as you are congratulating yourself on how well you prepared your children, on what a good fit the new child is in your family, on how smooth the adjustment has been, it will all come to an abrupt halt. It is usually something trivial that sets it off: a toy someone doesn't want to share, a shove, seemingly accidental. One of the children intrudes ever so slightly on the other's turf; noses are already out of joint because of favoritism, perceived on both sides, and suddenly the harmony and Sunday manners are gone. Your children are at each other's throats and you are wondering how it ever could have seemed like a good idea to have any children at all.

As stressful as your children's quarreling may be for all of you, the end of the honeymoon is a good sign that your children—old and new—are beginning to feel comfortable with one another. They can be themselves, show their real feelings, and be pretty sure that there will be no devastating results. If it looks as if they can handle it themselves, let them do it. Getting involved as a broker in your children's relationships is an invitation for the quarrels to escalate and makes you vulnerable to accusations of favoritism from both sides. Intervene only if they are badly mismatched or if something really ugly is developing.

When the quarrel is over, you can sit down with the children—individually or together—and reassure them that brothers and sisters do fight, that you expect it will happen from time to time, and that it is not the end of the world or their relationship with each other. They need to know that angry feelings and expression of those feelings are normal and sometimes necessary in families. Your job is not to get them to repress their anger, jealousy, or hurt but to teach them to express those feelings in ways that won't inflict long-lasting wounds (physical or emotional). Your newly adopted child may be particularly vulnerable to hurt feelings or fearful that quarreling will jeopardize her position in your family. She may need extra reassurance that it is safe for her to be honest about her feelings.

Fighting is only one thing brothers and sisters do together. They also spend a fair amount of time playing and working together, and you can help them use this to build ties between them. Encourage them to plan and work together on some project. Very small children might build something from Lego or construct a sand castle together; older children can do something more elaborate. They may even want to decorate the room they are sharing or rebuild the engine of an old car they have bought together. Give them a chance to teach each other a skill. Your roller skater may not have figured out how to knit, and that may be just the skill your other child has down pat. Your computer buff might want to exchange her expertise for a few tips on soccer playing.

The possibilities are limited only by the skills your children have or want to learn. If they both want to learn something—karate or ballet, for instance—they might enjoy learning it together. If they are both novices, neither will feel outdone by the other. You can offer guidance and quietly see to it that one sibling isn't always the one who shines, but for the most part, your children should discover for themselves the kind of activities they enjoy sharing.

Sometimes sharing activities they don't especially enjoy acts as a bond too. Doing chores together comes to mind here. They may gripe and complain—you can practically guarantee they will—but they will be griping and complaining on the same team. Working together can also be quite positive if they are doing real work that is clearly necessary to the family. When it is done, they will be able to share in the glory as well.

We sometimes like to think of our families as a unified group whose members are all more or less of like mind. That is only partially true. Families are also made up of groupings within the group and alliances of all sorts. An alliance familiar to us all is the children versus the parents. If your adopted child is going to be a full-fledged member of your family, she will need to be a member of the children's alliance and the other alliances within your family. Once she is comfortable with you, encourage her to spend time with her sisters and brothers—even if she would prefer to spend all her time with you. In the long run, it will be to her benefit and the family's if she builds strong bonds with everyone who is a part of it.

The Extended Family

Nuclear families—parents and their children—are a part of larger groups we call extended families. Grandparents, aunts, uncles, cousins, and assorted in-laws make up extended families, and while they don't usually live together, they are a vital part of most nuclear families. American families have become quite sophisticated about adoption. Generally, it is seen as one of two possible, and equally acceptable, ways to have children. Most grandparents are as delighted with an adopted grandchild as they are with one who has been born into the family, so long as that grandchild is a healthy white infant. It may be a little more difficult for extended family to accept a child who is older, handicapped, or interracial—and these are the very children who most need to be fully accepted into their families.

While no one in the twentieth century is likely to suggest that couples planning to adopt have their parents' permission, it does make good sense to discuss the possibility with them beforehand, both as a courtesy and as a way of sounding them out on their feelings about adoption and on the particular sort of child you have in mind. Their attitudes will have some effect on your child and on your whole family. If you can assess beforehand just how they are likely to feel, you will be better able to deal with any negativity. If your parents or other relations close to you are openly hostile to the idea of adoption or the adoption of a particular sort of child, you will have some soul-searching to do. You could have a situation on your hands that will require you to make choices between your child and some other members of your family.

If you already have children who are strongly attached to grandparents or aunts or uncles who are very negative to the adoption, then you have a real dilemma. What if someone close to you or close to your children absolutely refuses to accept the child you have adopted? Are you prepared to insist on acceptance as a condition of a relationship with any member of your family? Is it fair to the children you already have to risk the loss of relatives they dearly love in order to bring a new child into the family? Is it fair to your adopted child to continue relationships with family members who reject her? It certainly isn't fair to have your relatives dictate whether or not you can adopt a particular child, but in some circumstances, choosing to adopt could mean closing the door on other established relationships.

If you suspect that you are going to have a problem that will be difficult to resolve, you need to do some hard thinking, both within your household and within your larger family— and you need to do some hard praying as well. Ask your family to join you as you try to discern God's will for you in this. A family member who rejects a child because of her age, her racial background, a handicap, or simply because she is not in your bloodline, is not in a morally defensible position, but it does not follow that you should adopt the child you are considering simply because your family has taken a morally indefensible stance. God intends for families to be supportive communities where people can thrive emotionally and spiritually. If your family cannot be this sort of community for this child, she probably belongs in another family.

If you have adopted without discussing it beforehand with your family and you have been surprised by some negative or hostile attitudes, your responsibility is clear. You have committed yourself to this child. Neither she nor your other children would ever understand if you allowed a rejecting relative to prevent her from being happy in your home. You may have to cut off contact—temporarily, you would hope—with a relative whose behavior threatens to sabotage the adoption and the unity of your family—even if he or she has been a model uncle, aunt, or grandparent to your other children. Jesus warned us that we might have to reject our brothers or sisters or our parents if they interfere with our doing God's will (Matthew 10:35–37; Mark 10:29, 30; Luke 18:29, 30). It doesn't happen too often, but when it does, our moral responsibility is clear.

With any luck (and it may take much discussion and prayer to bring this luck about) you won't be facing these painful decisions when you adopt. Your family will support you, even if they don't quite understand what you are doing, and will take your child to their hearts. As in the case with brothers and sisters, it is best if you let your child forge bonds within the extended family in her own way and at her own pace. You can help the process along a little by sharing with your family some of the important information you have about her from the records or from your own observations. You may have noticed, for instance, that she draws well. She might enjoy meeting your sister-in-law who does pottery, or your great-aunt who designs quilts. The writer or librarian or avid reader in your family will enjoy her interest in books; the mechanic or carpenter will appreciate her facility with tools. Help your family see her gifts and let her get to know the gifts that are in your family as well.

You can prepare your child for her new extended family by sharing stories and pictures of them even before she has met them, perhaps even before she has moved into your home. And your family will be more at ease with her if they know her by sight and have a little of her history beforehand.

It is not necessary or even desirable to give out every detail that is in your child's record, but there are things that are important to share. If she has been abused, she may be very withdrawn around new adults. You can let your family know she has reason to feel cautious when she is meeting new people. If she was sexually abused, she may have a lot of trouble warming up to your father or your brothers. Let them know that they need to be very cautious in their approach to her, and they should not let their feelings be hurt if she isn't enthusiastic about them. It may take quite some time for her to feel safe around them. If your child is handicapped, telling your family about any adaptations they need to make for her will make the first meetings much more comfortable.

Once your child and your family have the information they need about each other and have gotten together a few times, you can step back and let the relationships develop. Keep an eye on things discreetly if you have any reason to believe that your child may not be accepted by some member of your family, but try to stay in the background, just as you have with your other children. Relationships are built one-on-one. An intermediary is more likely to build barriers instead of bridges.

Your Child and Her New Community

When your child comes to live with your family, nothing is familiar. Unless she is a babe in arms, she is going to have to make a great many adjustments all at the same time, and that is not going to be easy. More often than not, her new family comes equipped with a house, neighborhood, and potential playmates who are new to her. She will have a new doctor, a new dentist, new teachers in a new school, and a new pastor in a new church.

If you have shared your plans to adopt, you will have a pretty good idea of where it is going to be easiest for your child to make her transitions. When she has had a little while to get used to you and your household, begin to introduce her to some of the people who are going to be in her life from now on. It is all right to "stack the deck" by introducing her first to people you know will be welcoming and who don't pose any threat to her.

Unless there is a dire need for it, your daughter really doesn't have to start out her life with you by having her teeth cleaned or catching up on her immunizations. Let her meet the neighbors you are most friendly with, take her to church, and stay with her at Sunday school if she is reluctant to have you leave. Meet with her teachers, in Sunday school and in her regular classroom, before you bring her in. Prepare them for any special help she may need, but don't paint her as a difficult child. You want them to have the same optimism about her that you have.

If your child is noticeably "special," if she is handicapped or of a racial minority coming into a community that has been homogenous up to this point, you may need to do a little more preparation to ensure that she will be eased into the community comfortably. Make a point of talking with your neighbors, and sit down with her teachers and your pastor to explain any special accommodations she may need. There is a federal law that makes educating handicapped youngsters in a regular classroom mandatory if there is any way of managing that. The classroom teacher may not have had much experience teaching deaf or blind children or managing a child in a wheelchair in her classroom, but there will be somebody within the school system who is trained to do these things and to teach other people—the classroom teacher and her students among them—how to make the physical and communications adaptations they need to accommodate such a child. If this person can come to your child's classroom to prepare the teacher and the class before your child arrives, it will be much easier all around.

If you are adopting a child from overseas, you may need to arrange for a bilingual teacher in her classroom for the first several weeks. Again, there is a federal law, and a good many at the state and local levels, covering this sort of special-needs child. There are federal laws about education in racially mixed classrooms too, but in all-white communities you need more than laws to integrate a minority child. Talking to school officials ahead of time gives them the chance to discreetly introduce the topic in classrooms and among the faculty. There is a delicate balance between preparing people for the issues and creating a self-fulfilling prophecy. If you can approach it in a matter-of-fact way ("This is the kind of child we are adopting; here are some things that could come up, but we don't expect any big problems with this terrific child"), you are most likely to achieve your goal of smoothing her path and eliciting acceptance from your community.

After you have done this, your role once again is to step back. If your child is going to thrive emotionally, she needs to be able to form relationships on her own. She needs to be able to make friends, to work things out with her teacher, to become part of the community in her own right. You provide her with a home and family that supports her and encourages her growth. You arrange for her education and give her opportunities to learn skills outside the classroom. You see that she has a chance to make friends. You acquaint her with the Gospel and open up the possibility of a personal relationship between her and God.

You lay the groundwork. She has to build on it. Her style and pace may be different from yours. She may meet obstacles you hadn't anticipated or she may place obstacles in her own path. You can guide her and advise her. When it is necessary, you can protect her from people and things that could cause her harm, but in the end she will attach herself in her own way to both the community that is your family and to the community outside.

Twelve

Special Adoptions

There are special issues attached to each sort of adoption. The age of the child is one variable, but there are other factors that can complicate adoptions.

Sibling Adoption

Sibling groups are sometimes available for adoption. They come in all combinations, from the relatively straightforward set of twins to groups of eight or ten children. If there are more than three or four siblings (and sometimes if there are fewer), they may be separated to enhance their chances to be adopted, and that brings a whole new set of problems. When siblings are adopted separately, the families need to deal with issues of grief and separation or with relationships with two or more additional families—or sometimes with both. Almost by definition, sibling groups involve older children with all the issues that go along with them. Yet adopting siblings is very well suited to many families. One single mother jumped at the chance to adopt a brother and sister, knowing she would probably not have another chance to have both a son and a daughter. Many couples are attracted to a ready-made family, and this sort of adoption ensures that there will be brothers and sisters and gives the children a strong sense of connectedness that many adopted children don't have.

In the easiest form of sibling adoption, the adoption of infant twins (or triplets), the issues are scarcely different from adopting a single infant (apart from the extra work). It used to be fairly common to separate twins for adoption purposes, but that is hardly ever done now. When it is done, the results can be devastating and may last a lifetime.

Separating twins—even at birth—is a double loss for them. Just as they have come to know the sounds and rhythms of their mother's body in utero, they know each other's. Very often twins, especially identical twins, have an extraordinary psychic bond—possibly from having shared their intrauterine lives. In the case of identical twins it is very likely also because they are genetically identical. Separating twins at a later age is the same sort of loss for them as losing any other sibling—only more so—for all of the same reasons.

More commonly, siblings are different ages. The situation may be relatively straightforward, as in the case of a couple who adopted a child and were asked a year or so later to take a second baby born to the same biological parents, but usually the children have been through some sort of loss and may have been separated not only from their parents but also from each other. The more children in the group, the more likely it is that they have been through some hard times. The guidelines in earlier chapters for integrating children at each age level into the family still apply, but with siblings, there is not the luxury of absorbing one new child at a time or building entirely new relationships. Your children already have relationships with one another that are going to affect their relationships with other members of your family.

With any adopted child, it is important to get complete records. With sibling groups, it is even more important. Even before the children come, it makes sense to ask for as complete a written record as possible, to meet with the foster parents or caretakers if the children have been in a residential placement, and to meet with the children's therapists if they are in treatment. Find out in advance what each child's particular issues are and what the dynamics between them are like. If there is going to be contact with brothers and sisters elsewhere, try to meet with the families who have these children, and be sure the agencies know that you are open to meet with any families who may adopt your child's siblings later on.

Preadoption visits are common in any adoption involving older children. Try to arrange to have visits with each child alone as well as with all of them. If your children are old enough, you might want to sit down with them and their caretakers and/or therapists to discuss any problems they think they are likely to have in becoming part of your family. There is no way to guarantee smooth sailing. In fact, you can just about guarantee that there will be many a rough patch en route to becoming a family, but if you have adequate background information and enough time to get to know one another in advance, you will have a better idea of what sorts of supports you need to build into your family—and there will be fewer surprises.

Expect jealousy and quarreling. This goes with the territory of having brothers and sisters. It may be intensified for your children if they have had a lot of unmet needs earlier in life. You may also find that the adoptive sibling group initially closes ranks against any brothers and sisters already in the home—and vice versa. Even in the best of circumstances, children are threatened by the arrival of a new sister or brother. The arrival of more than one is even more threatening and if they are troubled, as at least some members of a sibling group are likely to be, the adjustment is that much harder. You will need the patience of Job and the wisdom of Solomon to steer your way through the early weeks, but if you manage to pass the tests your children administer with love and evenhandedness, you will find yourselves growing into a real family, all the more committed to each other for the difficulty you had getting there.

Family Projects Can Bring You Closer

One good way to blend your families into one united family is to have a joint project. It is best if this is a project new to all members of the family so no one begins at a disadvantage or feels as though they are being asked to participate in a project that properly belongs to the other part of the family. You can use the preplacement visits to try to figure out common interests, skills, or needs, then plan the project very soon after the children come to live with you. The kind of project is limited only by your imagination and resources. You might want to go camping or hiking together, plan a special trip, build a new room or a playhouse, learn how to ski together. Miniprojects in which one parent takes a child from the original family and one from the new group to a special outing or teaches them how to do something that is best done by two or more people are also useful for building bonds between the "old" siblings and the "new" ones. At first the new children may object to being separated—or they may jump at the chance. You don't want to weaken the bonds between them, but you don't want these bonds to be a hindrance to developing new bonds either.

Children much beyond toddlerhood need to feel that their contribution to the family is important. This is true whether they are adopted or homegrown. If they have been in a good residential program or foster home, they will already have had some responsibilities for the smooth running of their home. If they have come from a more chaotic background, it may take a while to get them used to the idea of participating in the family work. Starting with something fun like cooking or baking bread or building something the child is really interested in having is probably the best way to get started. The less interesting chores can be taught as you go along. Dishes will get washed and tables can be set as a part of the cooking project. Dusting, vacuuming, even painting and papering are less tedious if they are part of the job of fixing up a new room. Even the very young child can be helped to make her bed and find places for her special belongings as you settle her into a room (or a part of a room) that is her very own.

Doing chores together is a good way to build relationships between parent and child and between the old siblings and the new ones. Long ago, educator Maria Montessori demonstrated that children really enjoy doing work if it is appropriately structured to be challenging without being overwhelming and if it is "real" instead of "makework." Work gives children a sense of purpose and, carefully structured, it can be family building as well. For the family that has added two or more new children in one fell swoop, this can be a vital part of growing together as a family and a real practical necessity as well.

Contact With Absent Brothers and Sisters

In earlier times, it was thought that children adjusted best to new families if they broke all bonds to the old ones. Now we know that this is not necessarily true, that in many cases, having to choose between her old family and her new one put the adoptive child in an untenable position and made it hard—sometimes impossible—to be part of any family at all.

Before you adopt part of a sibling group, find out what sort of contact is planned and try to figure out what is going to meet the needs of your children. If you cannot accept your children's absent brothers and sisters as a real part of their family—and of yours—consider some other sort of adoption. It is an unbearable burden on a child to have to relinquish the love she has for one person or several to gain the love of another. Because she needs parents so much, she will probably try to accommodate you, but it is not fair, nor is it psychologically sound, to ask her to do this. If you have been able to meet the other brothers and sisters and their families (if they have been placed) ahead of time, you will have a better idea of what contact with this extended family is going to entail.

There are no rules for how often contact has to be made and what the nature of that contact should be, but at minimum, the children should have free access to each other by phone and letter and should have visits as often as they indicate the need. Holidays and birthdays are traditional times to get extended families of all kinds together, but you can plan other times as well, or instead. If the siblings live close enough, you can have them over for dinner some evening or take them along to a movie or a play. The siblings might enjoy going to the beach together, spending some time at summer camp, or playing on the same team.

Geography, resources, and the needs of all the children are going to determine the exact nature of their involvement with one another. What is important is your recognition that these children who don't live in your family are genuine siblings, just as the children who live together under your roof are. Family is not simply a group of people related by blood, marriage, or adoption. Our ideas about family have gone well beyond that in the twentieth century. If our families are going to be real homes for our children, we need to understand that.

Adopting the Handicapped Child

Years ago, handicapped children were simply written off as unadoptable. When Carl and Helen Doss wanted to adopt a child with a birthmark at midcentury, their agency, their families, and their neighbors thought they were crazy. It just wasn't done. But they persisted and their book *The Family Nobody Wanted* had an impact on the culture that went far beyond their own small world. We are all inspired by stories like that of the Doss family, or some of the more recent stories of families who adopt one handicapped child after another, but it is not an easy undertaking. Families who want to "rescue" a handicapped child by adoption should probably look for some other project.

A handicapped child, like any other child, needs primarily a family who will love her, accept her as she is, and encourage her to reach her realistic potential. She also needs special care physically, emotionally, or educationally, and sometimes a combination of these. Some children will need care throughout their lives. In many states, handicapped children can be adopted under a subsidy program that will take care of their medical bills. This makes adoption possible for many children who might earlier have been considered unadoptable.

If you are thinking about adopting a handicapped child, consider first what sort of handicap you would be comfortable with. The high-achieving, academically oriented family might not be able to raise a retarded child happily. The family whose primary pastime is skiing would probably feel tied down by a child with spina bifida, but each of these families might delight in a child who would be a trial for the other. It is important to be honest about your own limitations and your capacity to care for a particular sort of child. If you perceive your child as a burden rather than a joy, she will know it and you will have great difficulty growing together as a family.

As with any adoption, the attitude of your extended family is also a consideration. You may feel perfectly comfortable with a child who is deaf or has cerebral palsy, but if your parents or brothers and sisters don't, the adoption can become very complicated indeed. It is less of a problem if you don't already have children. Then you can determine the amount of involvement you are going to have with the extended family, but if you already have children who are attached to members of your extended family, you may need to consider whether your new child can be fully accepted and, if she is not, what sort of impact this will have on her and on your entire family.

Once you have decided that you do want to adopt a child with a handicap and you have figured out what sorts of handicaps you can comfortably manage, both emotionally and financially (in some cases you might have to modify your house to accommodate your child), get in touch with a parent group that concerns itself with this handicap. Talk to other parents, go to their meetings, read their newsletters and any other material you can get hold of. Talk with the specialists who would be caring for your child. Be sure all the supports you will need are, in fact, available to you before you bring your child home.

It seems like a lot of work ahead of time, but your child needs for you to be fully prepared to care for her and provide her with an accepting environment. Children who are defined as "hard to place" are involved in a disproportionate number of "failed adoptions." Careful preparation ahead of time can prevent this sort of painful failure for you and for your child, and allow you to get right to the real business of becoming a family.

The age-related guidelines for bonding are appropriate for handicapped children—sometimes with modifications. Your blind child will not be able to pick up visual signs; a child who is deaf will miss out on the auditory signals, and children with other sorts of handicaps may have difficulty perceiving or responding to some of your messages. You will have planned ahead for some of this; the nuances of interacting with your particular child will be learned "on the job."

Probably the biggest potential trouble spot in raising a handicapped child is expecting too little of her. She needs to feel she is a contributing member of the household. She needs to be able to "gripe" about her chores like the rest of the children, and her sisters and brothers need to see that she doesn't get unnecessary special treatment. Help her become competent in as many areas as she possibly can. Your other children may have good insights into ways you can help her learn. Include her in your family work projects and make sure the job, however small, is real work. Children know instinctively if we are giving them real responsibility or if we are only pretending.

A child with a handicap already knows she can't do some things that other children can do. Even more than other children, she needs to develop real competencies if she is going to feel good about herself. Adapt her responsibilities and her environment only as much as is really necessary. She will need to learn, within the framework of a loving and accepting family, that the outside world makes very few accommodations for handicaps. The most loving thing you can do for her, next to giving her a family, is to help her learn to function in such a way that she will be accepted by the outside world. You will, naturally enough, want to protect her from some of the harshness you see around you, but learn the difference between necessary protection and overprotectiveness.

Adopting an Interracial Child

Interracial adoption has become quite commonplace in the last three decades. The Dosses were pioneers in this department too. The Korean War also had an impact as American families rushed to adopt the orphans the war had made. Adopting war orphans was nothing new, but adopting orphans of minority or mixed race was. This experience opened the door to adoption for mixed-race American babies and, for a while during the 1960s and 1970s, adoption of racially mixed babies was very widespread. For a number of reasons that is no longer true.

In part, this has to do with the tendency of more single mothers, of all races, to raise their babies themselves. In part it is a rethinking of the philosophy behind interracial adoptions. Social workers in the Black community first raised the issue of whether a Black child could be adequately nurtured in a white home and community. This concern carried over to other minority communities, especially to the Native American community. The question of whether white parents raising a minority child can do justice to that child's racial heritage is an important one and has led to some serious study, within the white community, of racial heritages that make up the American people. Black History Month (February), for instance, gained quick and enthusiastic acceptance in this country, in part because so many families include interracial and minority members.

Another positive result of raising this question was a stronger effort within social service agencies to recruit minority parents for minority children. Families who had never thought of adoption were encouraged by the new openness of agencies to consider it, and many have, in fact, been able to adopt children. Adoption subsidies have helped families on limited incomes to adopt children they might in another time have fostered—formally or informally. But even with fairly aggressive recruitment programs, there have not been enough minority homes to accommodate the minority children available for adoption. Faced with a choice between permanent foster care or residential placement and adoptive placement in a family of a different race, most agencies are still opting for a permanent family for as many of their children as possible.

Interracial adoption is controversial, but in terms of a child's emotional growth and mental health, it is a defensible practice. The cautions are similar to the ones for any special child. It is vital that the child is wanted for herself, not as a symbol. The extended family has to be prepared to accept her wholeheartedly. If they aren't, the adoptive family needs to be prepared to stand behind their decision, perhaps even cut off contact with that portion of the family if they actively reject the child.

The adoption of a minority child may turn out to mean great sacrifices within the family, within the community, sometimes (subtly or not) on the job, and sadly, sometimes also within the church. Families contemplating an interracial adoption should test the waters in all areas of their lives that are important to them and be honest about how much support they will need to make the adoption possible. If they anticipate getting less support than they need, they should consider some other kind of adoption. Once they have adopted a child, that child needs their wholehearted commitment, even if they have to make some unanticipated sacrifices.

For all the realistic difficulties families face in interracial adoption, there are delights as well. The child herself is the primary delight—just as she is in any adoption. For parents who enjoy living with children, guiding them, and watching them grow, the child's gender and age, her racial or ethnic background, or any handicaps she may have, are likely to be only superficial concerns. Raising a child of a different race is an opportunity to educate ourselves about her heritage and to live, on a day-to-day basis, the reality that we are all sisters and brothers regardless of our outside covering. For the families who are called to this sort of adoption, it is a wonderful way of living.

International Adoption

With the shortage of American-born infants, more and more families are looking outside the country for their children. More than thirty years after the first Korean babies came to this country, they are still coming. From time to time, the Korean government restricts foreign adoption, but there has been a pretty steady stream of children since the 1950s. Vietnamese, Cambodian, Laotian, Indian, Bangladeshian, Haitian, and South American babies have enriched the lives of American families. Most internationally adopted children today are also interracial. Depending on which race you are talking about, they are more or less accepted by the communities into which they move.

International adoption is appealing because there is an abundant supply of children. Doors open and close in individual countries, but there are always babies and older children available somewhere. Infants are more likely to be available when you adopt overseas, but sometimes the red tape is so intricate that the baby assigned to you is no longer an infant by the time she gets to you. And not all babies billed as adoptable are, in fact, ready to be adopted. One mother went abroad with her other child to pick up the new baby, and wound up staying seven months while the birthmother was making up her mind.

In recent years international adoptions have been plagued with bouts of "baby selling" and placement of babies whose mothers have not agreed to adoption. It makes sense to investigate your agencies—both in the United States and in the country where you plan to adopt—thoroughly before you sign anything. An adoption-experienced attorney is essential to safeguard both you and your child.

International adoptions are expensive: ten thousand dollars and up. Some countries insist that you travel to pick the child up yourself; other countries will send them to the United States with an adult accompanying them. It is not uncommon to have all the paperwork done and a child assigned, only to have the country close the door to foreign adoption. Even a temporary closing can mean a permanent end to your plans to adopt a particular child.

Because most foreign adoptions involve Third World countries, you can expect that your child will come to you somewhat underdeveloped, undernourished, or ill (often with parasite infections). Try to get complete medical records, but be aware that you will probably have to play it by ear medically. Other parents who have adopted internationally can be very helpful in preparing you for your child. If there is a group of these parents in your area, try to get acquainted with them early in the application process. If you are not living near such a group, you can make contact by mail with one farther away. Most parent groups put out a newsletter and have people available to talk things over with you by phone or letter.

The more you know about your child's culture and the possible problems she may bring with her, the better prepared you will be to welcome her into your family. If you are prepared to handle the problems, they will be much less stressful for you and for your child, and you are much less likely to have an unexpected monkey wrench thrown into your first few weeks.

If your child is an infant, most of the guidelines for bonding to an infant will apply. With an older child, you may have an additional barrier of language to overcome. Once you know what country your child is coming from, try to learn some of her language. Most metropolitan areas offer courses in any language you might want to learn. If you don't live near enough to attend a course, a cassette course would be a good start.

When you learn your child's language and familiarize yourself with her culture, you are making an investment in your relationship with her. You are letting her know that her cultural heritage is a part of her that you value and that you would like her to value as well. Many parents of children adopted from overseas make a great effort to keep their children in touch with their heritage, to participate in the life of the ethnic community from which she comes, and to ensure that they and their children are well acquainted with the language. You will want her to learn English (and any other language you speak at home) and become familiar with your way of life as well, but the days are long past when we encouraged people to abandon their backgrounds if they wanted to be "real" Americans. We are more aware today that cultural diversity enriches American life and makes this a very special place to live.

You may find that an older child has not been a churchgoer and has little knowledge of the Gospel. If you are adopting from Asia or Africa, you are apt to have a child who not only knows little about the Gospel but who also has been acquainted with or practiced another faith entirely. Living in a Christian household is going to be quite an adjustment for her and will require tact, patience, and prayer on your part. Include her in your family devotions, bring her to church and share the Gospel with her, but don't push. She may derive a lot of comfort from the faith she came with for quite some time. Your job, with your adopted child and indeed, with any child you have, is to introduce her to the Gospel, to live a life that provides a good Christian witness for her and to pray for her. You can't give her faith. That is God's gift to her—in His own time.

Right now you may be getting the feeling that it would be a whole lot easier to adopt a healthy infant—and you would be right. It is easier (if you can find one), but easier isn't always better or even suitable. Adoptable children and the families who want them come in all styles. One sort of adoption will suit one family and quite another sort will suit another family that seems, on the surface, quite similar. Each adoptive family has the potential for helping a child, or several of them, blossom. Each child has the potential for bringing great joy into her family. There are no guarantees with adoption, just as there are none with homemade children, but we give our families a running chance if we have children for the right reasons, if we are honest with ourselves about what we can handle, and if we rely on God for our day-to-day support.

Thirteen

Unusual Circumstances

We usually think of adoption as an arrangement between adults and children who have had no previous relationship to each other, but in fact, a large percentage of the adoptions in the United States are intrafamily adoptions: the child and the adopting parent(s) are somehow related by blood or by marriage. The adoption either legalizes the current status or alters the sort of relationship they have within the family. Most commonly, a child is adopted within her family because of a parent's marriage—or remarriage. The children most likely to be adopted in this situation are children of widowed and never-married parents, but children whose parents are divorced are sometimes relinquished by the noncustodial parent, or that parent's rights may be legally terminated.

Stepparent Adoption

When a child has only one parent, there is a strong argument for adoption when that parent gets married. Adoption is formal recognition that the stepparent has made a commitment not only to the partner but also to the child(ren). It legalizes the day-to-day reality that they are a family, not just a couple with a dangling child between them. And it provides some security for the child in case her original parent dies or is unable to care for her.

Being orphaned is no longer as common in the late twentieth century as it was earlier, but it still happens. Some years ago, the mother of a young family died. Her husband remarried and, within a couple of years, he too died, leaving the three children in the care of their stepmother.

Because the stepmother had recently adopted the children, they had the assurance of a stable home. Her mother moved in with them so she could go to work, and together they made a family for children who, under different circumstances, might have lost every bit of security they had.

More recently, another family was not so fortunate. The father died just as the oldest of the four children hit the teens. The mother continued to raise the children, and in due course, remarried. Six months after the wedding, she was struck by a car and died. Her husband wanted to raise the children. The children wanted to stay with him, but an earlier will, never altered after the marriage, named another relative as custodian.

In the ensuing court battle, everybody lost. The stepfather lost his bid for custody and for visitation. The children lost not only the man they had begun to think of as "father" but each other as well. The older children, nearing adulthood, refused to live with the guardian. One of the younger children repeatedly ran away, and the youngest child was inconsolable as she lost one member of her family after another. Even the guardian, the apparent "winner," lost. She was bewildered and angry that her efforts to do what she thought was her duty went opposed and unappreciated.

This situation could have been avoided with an updated guardianship arrangement. Adoption is not only the way of ensuring security for a child who loses one or both of her parents. It is also a time-honored way that has many advantages. The child adopted by a stepparent may be more secure, both emotionally and practically. She will share the family's last name, she will not feel different, and she is assured of ongoing care if the biological parent dies. But the adoption can sometimes have drawbacks. Many widowed parents receive social security payments for themselves and their children. If their children are adopted by the new partner, those payments stop, and that can be a considerable financial loss to the family. This dilemma can be solved with a guardianship agreement in case the natural parent is unable to care for the children. The children may even use their stepfather's name informally and are in all but the technical sense "his" children as well as their mother's.

This sort of arrangement can be good in families in which the deceased parent's own parents are still very involved with their grandchildren and worry that adoption would end that relationship. In some families it may take time for the grandparents to be convinced that this will not happen, to be reassured that they are still a very much needed part of their grandchildren's lives. Only after they are reassured does the stepparent move to adopt the children.

In other families, the decision is made that the relationship with the grandparents is too important to jeopardize with a formal adoption. In still other families, the children are reluctant to be adopted—even when they have a good relationship with the stepparent—out of loyalty to the dead parent, because they don't want to change their name or for any of a dozen other reasons. When there has been a divorce, the reasons not to adopt are often even more compelling, and unless the noncustodial parent wants to relinquish his or her rights or has had them removed by the court, it is not possible to adopt, no matter how much the family might want that.

Still, stepparent adoption is fairly common and, as in any other adoption, there is really only one good reason to do it: because you want to be a parent to this child and raise her to adulthood. Any other reason, however "practical," that falls short of this is likely to lead to difficulty.

By necessity, building relationships is generally a long process, beginning with the time parent and stepparent were dating. Often the relationship has been developing for several years before adoption is considered. Like other adoptive relationships, these are built with shared time and activities, with communication and strong efforts to be in touch. Unlike other adoptive relationships, there is a significant difference in how the child sees and relates to each parent.

In standard adoption, both parents are new to the child. The child may see them as a unit and has no built-in reason to prefer one over the other. A stepparent is more than a new parent. She or he is likely to be seen as an interloper, an unnecessary intrusion on a relationship that was perfectly satisfactory from the child's point of view. The stepparent can count on having to overcome a good deal of resistance before the child accepts her or him as the natural parent's partner, and a good deal more before she is accepted as a second parent.

Our collective hearts are warmed by stories such as the one about Nancy Lincoln. Brought home unannounced by Abe Lincoln's widowed father, she took to the children, and was so accepted by them that Abe could say later in life, "All I am, I owe to my Angel Mother"—and mean Nancy, not the mother who gave birth to him. But for every Nancy and Abe Lincoln, there are hundreds of stepparents and stepchildren who have a much longer and more difficult adjustment to one another. Expecting too much too soon leads to disappointment and may prevent a really loving relationship from flourishing.

Intrafamily Adoption

Intrafamily adoption doesn't always involve a stepparent. Children are sometimes adopted by other blood relatives, most often by grandparents, aunts, uncles, or older brothers and sisters. When the natural parents have died, this is often the solution that makes the most sense and keeps the child feeling the most secure. Usually relationships have already been established. Adoption in these families only alters the legal status, not the relationship.

Sometimes, for reasons of money or family harmony, guardianship is a better idea than outright adoption. The financial issues are much the same as they are for a remarried widow with children. Adoption cancels the social security benefits. This can be a real consideration when the child is living with grandparents who are themselves, on a fixed income, or with other relatives who are raising families. Other relatives may object to an adoption if it looks as though it might jeopardize their relationship with the child.

Objections are most likely to come from the "other" side of the family. Paternal grandparents may be especially concerned if the adoption is going to involve changing the grandsons' surname. These may seem small concerns measured against the stability and security an adoption could offer to the child, but they need to be considered, especially if an adoption is going to involve more loss for the child. Maintaining as many family ties as possible may be crucial to the well-being of a child who has already lost both of her parents.

Full orphans are relatively rare in the late twentieth century. More often a child available for adoption has lost only one parent and has another who doesn't feel capable of caring for her—or she has two parents who, for one reason or another, cannot provide continual care for her. Intrafamily adoptions in these circumstances are of necessity open. The child will usually continue to have some contact with one or both natural parents.

Keeping relationships smooth in a situation that is, by definition, awkward, is the primary issue in this sort of adoption. When parents can't care for their children, there is usually a lot of guilt and anger on both sides. Relatives who "rescue" the children by adopting them need to be very sensitive to the emotional undertones. They need to balance the children's need for a stable home with a compassionate understanding for the parents who could not be parents. As much as possible they need to support their child's need—and the need of the natural parents—for some sort of contact with each other, without undermining their own roles as the legal and psychological parents.

The situation is like a divorce—only more so. Not only do the adoptive parents need to encourage their child's relationship with an absent parent (or two) but they also need to maintain their relationship with the natural parent. A divorce may create ex-spouses, but an adoption does not create ex-parents, ex-children, or ex-brothers and sisters. In an intrafamily adoption, juggling relationships is the name of the game.

Adoption as a Result of Infertility Treatments

Recent approaches to infertility treatment have given rise to a large number of children who are related biologically to only one of their parents. In many cases one—or sometimes both—parents may have to adopt the child to ensure that she is legally secure.

Artificial insemination is the older of these techniques, used when the husband is the infertile partner in a marriage; surrogate mothers are a fairly recent approach used when the wife is the infertile partner. Both approaches pose some moral problems for Christians.

In Old Testament times, both husbands and wives sometimes produced children who were not biologically their partner's child, and in some circumstances that was approved. For example, when a husband died without leaving children, it

150

was his brother's obligation to father children with the widow in the name of the dead man. When Onan resisted this, God killed him. When the wife was infertile, God sometimes allowed the husband to father children with another woman. Abraham's fathering of Ishmael with Hagar was done with Sarah's approval, and it fell within God's law for that time.

But that law has been altered in New Testament times. An adulterous union such as Abraham and Hagar's, or the polygamous arrangements that were often made when one brother fathered children in the name of his dead brother, are no longer acceptable. The modern-day dilemma is whether artificial insemination within a marriage or with a surrogate mother constitutes adultery. There is quite a lot of controversy and strong feeling among faithful Christians on this point. Probably the majority of Christians lean away from these routes to parenthood, but the issue is by no means clear-cut, and there are many Christian families who have used one form or the other to have a baby. In vitro fertilization raises some similar moral issues, but they are beyond the scope of this book.

In addition to the moral issues, pregnancies in which only one marriage partner is the biological parent bring up numerous psychological issues. We are most familiar with pregnancies which occur when the wife of an infertile husband conceives with the aid of an anonymous donor. Millions of babies have been born in this way and, for the most part, the circumstances of conception are not known beyond the family circle. Often only the couple knows the truth. In theory this offers infertile couples a simple, discreet way to become parents without publicizing their infertility, without depriving the wife of an opportunity to experience pregnancy and birth, and without going through the sometimes frustrating experience of proving their parent-worthiness to an adoption agency.

In practice it has not been so simple. There are potential problems that can put the whole family at risk. Husbands have sometimes underestimated just how strongly they would resent their wives having a child who was not biologically theirs, how difficult it would be to see a daily reminder of their infertility and to feel like a father to the child. Jealousy, anger, resentment, low self-esteem, and guilt can overshadow any positive feelings about a baby who was, at the outset, wanted and planned for. Physicians who practice artificial insemination try to screen for this and discourage couples whom they think might run into trouble.

If the husband is not entirely sterile, many physicians will inseminate with a mix of sperm from both the husband and the donor to allow some possibility for the husband to be the biological father. But biological father or not, the husband in a family that chooses this form of conception is the legal father and is expected to be the "real" (psychological) father as well. For a variety of reasons, that often proves to be more difficult than anyone ever imagined, and if it is not resolved the child and the marriage will suffer.

Once a baby has been conceived, it is too late to worry about the morality or the psychological wisdom of the decision. The parents may want to reconsider adding any further babies in this way, and there may be some things they need to work out with their consciences, but when a baby is on the way—or has already arrived—she is entitled to be welcomed and loved by both of the adults who made the decision to conceive her. If unexpected issues have come up, then counseling and/or healing is in order. Shame that you have done something you now think may be morally wrong, or embarrassment that you feel quite differently about your choice than you expected to (or than everyone else expects you to), is not a reason not to seek help. There is probably nothing you can tell a good counselor or healing minister that hasn't been heard before. Pastoral counselors and healers are trained to be both compassionate and discreet. If the person you have chosen seems more interested in berating you than in helping you and your family heal and grow together, find someone else.

The legal position of these children varies from state to

state. In some states they are not considered legitimate unless the husband adopts them. In other states, the husband is automatically the legal father. In most families, the legal issue doesn't come up unless there is a divorce. Many couples go to one physician for conception and another one for prenatal care to protect their privacy. Given the strong negative feeling that artificial insemination often calls forth, discretion is probably the most sensible approach.

Whether the child herself should know depends a lot on how the parents feel about their decision, on how many people already know, and on the risk of accidental discovery. There have been many instances of biology students in junior and senior high school realizing, when they studied blood typing, that their fathers could not be their biological fathers. Cautious physicians usually try to match blood types to avoid this, but there can be slipups.

A new and ominous problem with artificial insemination has recently appeared on the scene. There are reports of babies conceived in this way being born with AIDS. One of the few certainties that we have about AIDS is that it is transmitted via both blood and sperm. Anonymous donors, who have been largely unscreened for AIDS until recently, quite suddenly pose an enormous potential risk to their as-yet unconceived and unborn children. For many families, the risk may simply be unacceptable. Already, many couples are deciding against anonymous donors in favor of donors known to them. This minimizes the medical risks but may well increase both the legal and moral complications.

Finally, children conceived via artificial insemination share with adopted children the little-publicized risk of accidentally contracting incestuous marriages. For adopted children this risk could be eliminated by copying the German system of issuing original birth certificates to the adoptive parents at the time of adoption. For ordinary use, the birth certificate with the adoptive parents' name is used, but when the adopted child is married, the original birth certificate is required. This automatically ensures that no one accidentally marries a brother or sister or other close relative. Countries which do not exercise this caution have occasional well-publicized cases of closely related couples learning long after the fact—often after they have had children—that they are blood relatives. The risk for children conceived by artificial insemination is probably much higher because one donor may be used for conceiving a large number of children and tracking down the biological father's identity is even more difficult than finding the biological parents of an adopted child.

Surrogate mothering eliminates some of the problems of conception by artificial insemination, but creates some new problems of its own. Under this system, a woman of proven fertility volunteers to carry the child of a married man (conception by artificial insemination), then gives the baby up to be adopted by the man and his (usually) infertile wife.

Because medical screening is generally pretty rigorous, the medical risks are less significant than they are with standard artificial insemination, but the legal and psychological risks increase astronomically. For starters, there is the risk that the child may not be the child of the supposed father at all, but rather of the surrogate mother's husband. Despite written assurances, couples involved in this sort of project don't always abide by their promises to be celibate until a pregnancy has been confirmed. A highly publicized case involving a severely handicapped child had to be settled in the courts. There have also been cases of surrogate mothers deciding against relinquishing their babies. At least one woman has been involved in a custody battle over her as-yet-unborn child. In her recent book *Mothers on Trial* (McGraw-Hill, 1985), Phyllis Chesler suggests a number of frightening possibilities.

What happens if a surrogate mother subsequently discovers she can have no more genetic children of her own? Would she be entitled to visitation or custody of the child she gave away? What would happen if a couple had a child by a surrogate mother and later divorced? Who would be the child's legal and financial custodian?

Could the genetic father force a surrogate mother to abort? Could he refuse to honor his financial obligation to her or the infant if she refused to have the abortion? Could he successfully be sued for child support? By whom?

Attributing the popularity of surrogate motherhood to "women's economic poverty, male genetic narcissism, and the greed of lawyers, physicians, and other 'middlemen,' " Phyllis Chesler minces no words about the possible negative consequences, but even the observer whose opposition is less intense than hers is apt to have many questions, not only about the legal consequences but also about the psychological and moral consequences of such an arrangement.

Psychologically, surrogate mothering is a very different business from standard artificial insemination because the surrogate mother contributes more than genetic material to the process. Pregnancy and birth involve a full-time, nine-month commitment of a woman's physical, psychological, and spiritual resources. Relinquishing her baby is just as much of a wrench as it is for any other woman who gives up her child. It is bewildering that a society which is beginning to recognize the great loss birthmothers experience when relinquishing their children for adoption, simultaneously extols the surrogate mother, tells her she is doing a wonderful thing, and does not expect her or her family to have any grief or second thoughts. The baby too loses the mother whose voice and body rhythms are familiar to her.

As we learn more about the emotional life of an unborn baby, we need to wonder more and more about the lifelong effects on a child whose natural mother has distanced herself emotionally from the moment of conception, about the effects of stress throughout the pregnancy (for even in the best of circumstances, this is a stressful sort of experience), about the wisdom of deliberately conceiving babies who will be separated from the mothers who carry them. Knowing what we know about the generalized anxiety and the low self-esteem in adopted children, is it morally right to deliberately create a group of children for adoption?

Because most surrogate mothers have other children, we need to wonder about the effects on these children when their "sisters" and "brothers" are handed over—apparently with no regrets. What do they think about their mothers' commitment to them? Could they just as easily be given up? What is the effect on little girls of seeing their mothers pregnant with a child they insist is not really theirs? Can a woman carry a child for a friend or a relative or a stranger without losing some of her own capacity to love and commit herself to other people?

The moral issue of adultery is as much an issue in surrogate mothering as it is in pregnancies by artificial insemination— and legally, it is more of an issue. Most states do not recognize the biological father as the real father. The legal parents (surrogate mother and her husband) have to relinquish the baby, and in most cases the biological father and his wife have to go through adoption proceedings.

One of the forgotten people in the surrogate-mother controversy is the wife of the biological father. She may have yearned for a baby as much or more than her husband. Infertility for her means the loss not only of the possibility of having a child that is biologically hers but also the loss of the experiences of pregnancy and birth that are so central to women's lives—experiences that her husband would not, in any case, have had.

While many couples say they have decided on surrogate parenting because of the extreme shortage of adoptable babies, in most cases this decision is made, in part at least, because of the husband's desire for a child who is biologically his and/or his resistance to raising an adopted child.

Jealousy, anger, resentment, low self-esteem, and guilt are just as likely to afflict the woman whose husband is producing a baby with a surrogate as they are to afflict the husband whose wife is pregnant by artificial insemination. And because the primary caretaker in most families continues to be the mother, her feelings are even more likely to have a negative impact on the baby. Because she is not the biological mother, she may also feel (and actually be) at some disadvantage should she ever be divorced. Would there be any chance at all for her to have custody of this child whom she has raised from infancy?

Some families have children both by adoption and by surrogate mothers, and this is perhaps the most difficult situation of all. What can adopted children possibly think if their father feels cheated because he hasn't had a biological child? The story of Jacob, Leah, and Rachel in the Old Testament is an analogous situation. Jacob had plenty of biological children— ten sons and probably some daughters by his wife Leah—but Leah wasn't the woman he loved and wanted to have children by. Because he was an honorable man, Jacob stayed with Leah, even though her father had tricked him into marriage. He had children with her, but he felt cheated.

When Jacob was finally able to marry Leah's sister, Rachel, the woman he really loved, he also had children with her. His love and preference for their first child together, Joseph, was legendary—and not surprisingly, it stirred up considerable resentment among his other children, with disastrous results for the whole family. Modern-day siblings may have more subtle ways than Joseph's brothers did to express their resentment, or they may simply turn all the resentment inward and become depressed. In any case, going to such lengths to create a child who is in a unique way the father's "own" is not likely to make family life more harmonious.

Couples who, despite the drawbacks, have gone ahead with surrogate mothering and have had second thoughts will need to face a number of issues in a responsible way. Should they offer to let the surrogate mother keep the child and pay child support to her? If that is not feasible, should they offer visitation to her and the siblings? If it looks as though it will be difficult for the adopting mother to be mother to a child who is expected or already in the home, then counseling and/or healing is in order—for the baby's sake, for the sake of the adults who will raise her, and for the sake of the marriage.

Surrogate mothering sometimes leads to some form of open adoption. If the surrogate mother is a sister or close relation to the adopting mother, there is invariably some kind of ongoing contact. In the case of stepparent and relative adoption, some continuing relationship with the biological parent(s) is almost a given. And, more and more, nonrelative adoptions have some degree of openness.

Open Adoption

Open adoption first gained popularity when the child being adopted was older or part of a sibling group that was not being adopted together. Social workers and adoptive families recognized the importance to these children of maintaining ties with at least some members of their original families, and the adoptions were arranged with these contacts in mind. While there were, inevitably, some snags, open adoptions in these families generally worked fairly well because everybody had agreed to this sort of adoption from the outset.

As the supply of adoptable babies diminished and birthmothers began to be more aware of their own need to be involved in the adoption process, open adoptions of various sorts began to be planned for newborns and small children. In some cases, that openness meant that the birthmother was allowed to select, from a number of anonymous case histories, the family she thought would be most suited to her baby. A face-to-face meeting might be arranged at the adoption agency, and an agreement to send pictures and developmental reports for several months or a year might be incorporated into the adoption.

Private adoptions might include even more contact as the birthmother and the adopting couple seek each other out.

These families often exchange names, addresses, and phone numbers. Quite a few adopting couples are invited to attend the birth and even go to childbirth classes with the birthmother. Postadoption contact ranges from none at all to regularly scheduled visits. Suzanne Arms, in *To Love and Let Go* (Knopf, 1983), explores in photographs and a very moving text the variety of experiences families can have with the open adoption of a newborn.

Adoptions can also become open when the biological and adoptive families make contact with each other. Most of these contacts are initiated by the biological family and they are sometimes quite upsetting for the adoptive family, which had expected complete confidentiality. Less often, the adoptive family makes the first move, usually—but not always—to the delight of the biological mother (and sometimes her family too). What both biological and adoptive families need to realize is that there is no such thing as absolute confidentiality of adoption records. Rarely are they as inaccessible and "sealed" as families imagine they are. They are generally inaccessible only to the concerned parties: the biological and adoptive parents and the adoptee herself. A little discreet sleuthing usually turns up enough information to make a search.

A generation ago, adoptive families seldom thought about the possibility of contact with their children's biological parents (though I believe adoptees have thought about their original parents more than their adoptive families ever imagined). Today's adoptive families need to expect the possibility of some sort of contact at some time in their children's lives. The biological parent may search, the adoptee may search, and even the adoptive parents may decide there is good reason to have contact between the families.

In most cases, when contact between the families is made, it is the biological parent who does the searching. Women in the last quarter of the twentieth century are beginning to realize that having a child alone is no longer thought of as the next worse thing to ax murder. Raising a child alone is far from an impossible task. If these women are of the generation that routinely signed on the dotted line and were told to go home and forget it, they may feel terribly cheated as they watch women in similar circumstances who, only a few years later, kept their children and were able to have the joy of raising them. They grieve over their lost children and long to see them.

While most birthmothers who search follow the advice of search groups to wait until their children are eighteen, some search earlier. Most of these women do not make direct contact with underage children. They may be satisfied just to know the children are in good hands, or they might make contact with the adoptive parents instead.

Adoptive parents may worry needlessly about this contact. For the most part, birthmothers are conventional women with backgrounds similar to the adoptive parents'. The overwhelming majority of them had babies when they were too young to be mothers, or they were in situations in which there was no support. Many of them grow up, marry and have more children. They are our neighbors, our friends, members of our own families. Almost to a woman, they are concerned first with the welfare of the children they relinquished, and they don't want to do anything to disrupt their lives.

If your child's birthmother contacts you, you could ask her not to make contact again or you could meet her for tea and get to know this woman who brought your child into the world. As your child's parent, it is up to you to decide if contact should be limited to an occasional letter or phone call between the adults. Sometimes there is room in the family circle to include the birthmother. If the situation arises, the adoptive parents are the people most likely to know what best meets the needs of their child and their family.

Just as often the adoptee initiates the search. She may wait until she is an adult, or she may already be eager to look when she is an adolescent. Many adoptive parents who would be willing to help with a search once their child is eighteen balk at helping their adolescent, but that may be just the time when she needs to know about her heritage so she can find out about herself. We don't know why some adopted children struggle more with the issue of identity than others do. It usually doesn't have much to do with the kind of parenting they have had but rather with their internal makeup. People who are raised in the families in which they are born may have a lot of difficulty understanding how much some adoptees yearn to be in touch with their backgrounds, to feel connected in the way that other people take for granted. Helping them fill in some of the blanks may make it easier for them to make peace with themselves.

Adoptive parents often worry that their children who search don't love them or that they will come to love the birthparents more. If your relationship has been reasonably good, there is no reason to believe a search will alter that. If anything, your child may love you more for your support and may see both you and her birthparents more realistically later on. The biological parent is an important link to the adoptee's background—there might even be potential for a warm relationship to develop—but the adoptive parents are the psychological parents, the "real" parents with whom the child has the strongest bond. There is no great risk of unraveling that tie with a search.

Occasionally, the adoptive parents will make the initial contact because there is information they need for their child's health care, because they recognize their child's need to know more or to make contact, or because they want to share the delight of their child. There have been some highly publicized cases in which the biological family has rejected any contact—even to share much-needed medical information. Some birthmothers fear or reject contact because their families object or never knew about their babies, but most birthmothers are delighted with and grateful for the adoptive parents' initiative.

161

Contact doesn't inevitably lead to an ongoing relationship, but it may lay to rest some questions and fears for all members of the adoption triangle.

Single-Parent Adoptions

Single-parent adoptions—in the formal sense—used to be out of the question, though for generations single women have made informal agreements to raise other people's children.

It wasn't until the late 1960s that agencies began to experiment seriously with placing children with singles. These adoptions were generally last-resort placements for last-resort kids: the older, minority, or special-needs youngsters who hadn't been able to get a place in a two-parent family.

In their 1977 article in *Social Casework*, William Feigelman and Arnold R. Silverman comment on the curious practice that "those who are felt to possess the least resources to parent have been assigned the children who would seem to require the most demanding kinds of care." But despite the clear implication that single-parent adoption was second rate, these families thrived, for the most part, and more singles clamored to be considered as adoptive parents.

There are some built-in advantages to having singles as adoptive parents. Adoption, for them, is nearly always a first-choice route to parenthood. Singles don't adopt children to hold together shaky marriages—an all-too-common practice in the married world. Single parenthood for them does not carry a legacy of grief and anger as it might for the divorced, widowed, or never-married parent. For many of the children adopted, the simple one-to-one relationship in a single-parent household offers the best chance they have of making an attachment and of having the concentrated attention they so badly need.

The adoption process for singles is much like it is for couples, only harder. "Even though the law forbids discrimination on the basis of marital status, some agencies are not really open to single parents adopting," one mother notes. She got involved with a network for single adoptive parents before she applied to adopt, and that network "helped me steer clear of agencies that did not welcome single applicants." It took a couple of years, but this mother eventually adopted an infant son from South America.

Sometimes the agency finds the children. Other parents have to locate their babies themselves. The Adoption Resource Exchange of North America (ARENA) can facilitate that with some domestic adoptions. They maintain files and albums on adoptable children, usually considered hard-to-place, all over the country. Foreign babies can be difficult and expensive to locate. Single parents and couples go through roughly the same expense, bureaucratic snarls, and waiting when the adoption is an international one.

Adoption doesn't end once the child arrives. The real work and joy are just beginning. The move from single person to single parent dictates a number of new practical considerations, most obviously child care. Many adoptive parents try to arrange some maternity/paternity leave at first. Some parents can take their children to work, others choose to work at home.

Single adoptive parents may depend heavily on extended family for support. Agencies may even consider the family support available in making a decision about placement. Other parents have found their support among their friends or in more formal groups of single parents. The key to making it work is having a support network in place before the child comes—whether it is family, friends, or neighbors—because you are doing it alone.

Is it worth it? "It is real draining," says one father. "After four teenagers, I don't have as much energy, but it's been important to me and to my sons to *be* a family."

Another single mother is unequivocally positive. "I'm so happy that even when I get exhausted, I don't feel depleted. There's something about wanting something, getting it, and finding it *is* what you want. I don't have any sense that I have it hard and other people have it easy."

Clearly, too, the children benefit from having a home. The younger ones take it for granted, but the older children can articulate the differences in their lives before and after adoption. One teenager lived in a group home before he was adopted. "Now I get all the attention. Dad spends a lot of time with me. He helps me with my homework. I think I have a pretty good time with him."

For these parents and a few thousand like them, adoption has focused their lives and given them purpose. The children have a home, family, and perhaps siblings they might not otherwise have had. If these homes differ from society's "ideal," so do other homes.

Single-parent adoption is one of the many new forms of adoption. Some of these new forms solve problems that seemed unsolvable in earlier times. Some of them create a new set of problems along with the solutions, but they are all a response to the challenge of the late twentieth century: to create families for the children and adults who want to be in them.

Fourteen

What Is
a Family?

Ask most people to define *family* and they will probably agree with the dictionary that a family is "all the people living in the same house" or "all those descended from a common ancestor" (*Webster's New World Dictionary*), but in practice, it is much broader than that. We routinely include people related by marriage and by adoption. We speak of our "church family"; neighborhoods form family clusters and our closest friends are "just like family."

When "Outsiders" Are Part of Your Family

As adoption practices change, our notion of family changes with them. Family certainly includes the idea of "parents and their children" and "all the people living in the same house." This is the grouping we call "nuclear family." But even in the

165

traditional nuclear family—a couple and the children born to them—all of the members weren't descended from a common ancestor. Except in the dawn of history, two different sets of ancestors combined to form each new nuclear family. One partner—generally the wife—was "adopted," and the family was identified with one lineage only.

Adopted children add new sets of ancestors and, more and more, new living relatives to the family constellation. Even in the traditional "closed" adoption, where there is no contact between biological and adoptive families, families no longer try to maintain the fiction that their adopted child came unencumbered into the world. The biological relatives form a kind of extended "phantom family." You know they are there even if you have never seen them.

In many adoptive families, the biological family has more than a phantom existence and plays some role in the family's life. A kind of new-fashioned in-law, these relatives have the same general advantages and disadvantages as other, more standard relatives. You may welcome them as part of your family or you may merely tolerate them for your child's sake.

Whatever the degree of closeness, once it has been decided that your child would benefit from contact with her biological family, it is up to the adults to see that that works smoothly. The criterion of involvement of the biological family is the well-being of the child. There are good reasons not to involve them: If the child has been abused in the past, if the biological parent is extremely unstable, or if it seems likely that the adoption would be sabotaged by this sort of contact, then it makes sense to restrict it or rule it out altogether. Practically speaking, in most families, it is not apt to be an issue while the child is growing up.

Open adoption continues to be a voluntary arrangement that is usually negotiated before the adoption takes place. Biological and adoptive families who are not interested in such an arrangement don't ordinarily enter into it. Occasionally, one family (more often than not the biological family) will decide sometime after the adoption to make contact, and the issue of contact with the child will have to be negotiated at this point. The adoptive family holds the legal cards, but this decision, like any other, should be determined by the child's best interests rather than by legal concerns.

In any family, the children may love someone whom their parents (or one parent) don't much care for. Unless that person poses a real danger to the child, the relationship should not be discouraged. Other people have much to give our children—even those people we have a hard time appreciating. Our time together with our children is short and too precious to waste arguing over the people they choose to love. If they are very young, or passive, they may give in and lose a person who might have been a good support. More often, their affections go underground. They may maintain a relationship surreptitiously, and they will most certainly be resentful of us for putting them in the midst of such a painful dilemma.

Our children need to know that we respect their need to love and be loved by people other than ourselves. They need to feel secure that we will protect them from anyone who might hurt them (even when they don't want to be protected) and to trust that we won't confuse genuine protectiveness with jealousy. We are, after all, building families, not private armies.

Maintaining a Family Atmosphere

Family building involves creating atmospheres in our homes that nurture the children and adults who live in them. A certain amount of time needs to be devoted to maintenance (earning money and cleaning house, for instance), and a certain amount of time is needed to acquaint our children with the rules of the society they live in, and to help them develop their character, but there has to be more if children and parents are going to want to be part of the same family.

Our time together has to be fulfilling—not always fun, but

productive. There is no end to the kind of activities families can do together. Interest, skill, and resources determine the pursuits each family will share. The time for these pursuits is now. Children have a way of growing up while their parents say, "As soon as we have time. . . ." If you have adopted an older child, your time together will be even shorter—and more precious—than it is with children who join your family in infancy.

No family has enough time to wait until they "get out from under." Planning something to do together on even the busiest day—breakfast, a quick cup of tea, a run around the block, or a chapter of your favorite reading-aloud book—helps everyone keep in mind why it is that we are all living together in the first place. Families who pray and read God's Word together are reminded that they have been called together, not only as members of their own household but also as members of God's larger Christian family.

Prayer Always Helps

God's hand in creating a family is sometimes easier to see in the adoptive family. We have grown accustomed to the ongoing miracle of creating new life. Most twentieth-century families expect to be able to produce a baby whenever they choose, and they aren't very surprised when a baby is conceived or born healthy. What surprises us, sets us back on our ears, and reminds us that we are not the principal creators, is the inability of modern medicine to ensure a baby for every family that wants one.

The realization that we are dependent on God, and the people He chooses to work through, for a child is the beginning of awareness of just how much a miracle and a privilege it is to be a parent. Some prayer and introspection helps many adults move from thinking about how much their family needs a child to thinking about children who need to be part of a family. A good many couples will still want a baby or very young child, but some couples will feel drawn to an older or special-needs child.

The key to searching for a child who will fit into your family is prayer and reflection. Ordinarily, God works through the dictates of our hearts. Only rarely are we asked to choose a way of life that "goes against the grain," and in those cases, God speaks so clearly to us that there can be no mistaking the message. Don't go looking for a handicapped child, a sibling group, or a ten-year-old if you really want a healthy infant. Your child needs to be wanted for herself. If you select a child out of guilt or a sense of duty, you are probably not listening carefully to God's voice within you, and you are creating a setup for adoption failure. Parenthood, even when you have the children you had hoped for, has all the built-in sacrifices you could ever want, and there are plenty of surprises along the way. These surprises and sacrifices are much easier to handle if you start out with the kind of child you really want.

This is not to say that the end result will be exactly what you had in mind. All children turn out differently from what we expected. Our swaggering two-year-old becomes a re-served history professor. Our delicate ballerina dons heavy boots and works at an archaeological dig. The brightest of our children drops out of school and hitchhikes across the coun-try; a shy bookworm is transformed into a union organizer. Some children exceed our ambitions for them; others fall far short.

We all have dreams—some very general, others quite spe-cific—for our children. They may delight or disappoint us; they may do us proud or embarrass us. We may be heartened, or hurt, by the kind of people they become. Almost certainly we will be surprised, because we cannot possibly anticipate the variety in the gifts and potential of any one child. As par-ents, we do our best to encourage the potential in our children and to help them develop good character traits. Usually our efforts pay off, but there are no guarantees.

Parenthood is an art—and a complicated one at that—because the fashioning of a human being requires at least two artisans: a parent and the child herself. Our efforts are important, but the outcome is never totally our doing. Parenthood is an act of faith.

We are called to bring children into our families—by birth, by adoption, and in some families, by both routes. Once we have opened our hearts and our homes to children, we are responsible for their well-being, for nurturing them physically, emotionally, and spiritually. It is the most demanding job we will ever undertake. A measure of our success when we have finished the job is their ability to take care of themselves and our ability to let them go.

The ties we have with our children stretch and change shape and might even seem to disappear. Sometimes they break altogether. More often they are pulled into a circle that binds us together in a new and lasting way. It is what we all hope for, but these love ties are built slowly, with patience, persistence, and prayer.

For Further Reference

Anderson, David C. *Children of Special Value*. New York: St. Martin's Press, 1972.

Arms, Suzanne. *To Love and Let Go*. New York: Alfred A. Knopf, Inc., 1983.

Berends, Polly. *Whole Child–Whole Parent*. New York: Harper's Magazine Press, 1975.

Bumgarner, Norma J. *Helping Love Grow: Some Hints for Mothering Your Adopted Baby*. Franklin Park, Illinois: La Leche League, 1974.

Chesler, Phyllis. *Mothers on Trial*. New York: McGraw-Hill Book Company, 1983.

Doss, Helen. *The Family Nobody Wanted*. Boston: Little, Brown, 1954.

Gribben, Trish. *Pyjamas Don't Matter*. Auckland, New Zealand: Heinemann Educational Books, 1979.

Jones, Sandy. *Crying Baby, Sleepless Nights*. New York: Warner Books, 1983.

———. *To Love a Baby*. Boston: Houghton Mifflin, 1981.

Kersey, Katharine C., Ed. D. *Sensitive Parenting*. Washington, D.C.: Acropolis Books, LTD, 1983.

Kirk, H. David. *Adoptive Kinship: A Modern Institution in Need of Reform*. Toronto: Butterworths, 1981.

———. *Shared Fate*. New York: The Free Press, 1964.

Klaus, Marshall H. and Kennell, John H. *Maternal-Infant Bonding.* St. Louis: C. V. Mosby Co., 1976.

Klaus, Marshall H. and Klaus, Phyllis H. *The Amazing Newborn.* Reading, Massachusetts: Addison-Wesley, 1985.

Of Cradles and Careers. Franklin Park, Illinois: La Leche League International, 1983.

The Heart Has Its Own Reasons. Franklin Park, Illinois: La Leche League International, 1984.

The Womanly Art of Breast-Feeding. Franklin Park, Illinois: La Leche League International, 1981.

Leboyer, Frederick. *Loving Hands.* New York: Alfred A. Knopf, 1976.

LeShan, Eda. *The Conspiracy Against Childhood.* New York: Atheneum Publishers, 1967.

————. *When Your Child Drives You Crazy.* New York: St. Martin's Press, 1985.

Liedloff, Jean. *The Continuum Concept.* London: Gerald Duckworth & Company, LTD, 1975.

Lifton, Betty J. *Lost and Found.* New York: The Dial Press, 1979.

————. *Twice Born: Memoirs of an Adopted Daughter.* New York: McGraw-Hill, 1975.